Gluten-Free
Baking
Classics

ANNALISE G. ROBERTS

SURREY BOOKS
CHICAGO

Edited by Bookcrafters, Inc., Chicago
Designed and typeset by Joan Sommers Design, Chicago
Photographs on pages vi, viii, 14, and 142 © Tom DiBella
Printed in Canada.
Some recipes were originally published in *Gourmet Magazine*
Excerpts from Chapter 2 first appeared on www.foodphilosopher.com by
Annalise Roberts and Claudia Pillow

5 4 3

Library of Congress Cataloging-in-Publication Data
Roberts, Annalise G.
    Gluten-free baking classics / Annalise G. Roberts ;
foreword by Peter H.R. Green.— 1st U.S. ed.
        p. cm.
        Includes index.
        ISBN-13: 978-1-57284-081-2
        ISBN-10: 1-57284-081-1
    1. Gluten-free diet—Recipes. 2. Baking. I. Title.

RM237.86.R58 2006
641.5'638—dc22
                                2006002196

Surrey Books is an imprint of Agate Publishing, Inc.
Agate and Surrey books are available in bulk at discount prices.
For more information, visit agatepublishing.com

To Conrad—
Who made it possible for me to take my own "road not taken"

ACKNOWLEDGMENTS

Love and thanks to my sister Claudia for joining me as we bring our Food Philosopher dreams to life.

Thanks to Susan Schwartz, my publisher, for seeing the value and potential of my work.

Thanks to Gene DeRoin, my editor, who crafted a beautiful book from all those electronic documents and to Joan Sommers whose design flair made it all look so good.

Thanks to Tom DiBella, the food photographer who gave his exceptional creative skills and technical talent to this project. Your dedication touched my heart.

Thanks to Ruth Reichl and her staff at *Gourmet Magazine* who tasted my cupcakes and cookies and gave me a chance to share them with their readers.

Thanks to Shelly, David, Jack, and Rivka—your caring made all the difference.

A giant gluten-free thank you to my many willing testers, especially Alex and Bradford, Herb and Ev, Tim, Cory, and Monica, Don and Macie, Susan and Fritz Zeigler, Daria Ewanik, Mary and Greg Frazier, the whole Loretti clan, the Krafts, the Scheinerts, Vicki Hunt and her family, Carl Scariatti, and all the others I recruited and fed and questioned endlessly until I got it right.

To Evan Fogelman for all his enthusiasm, support, and efforts on my behalf.

To Sean Budlong, my website wizard for all of his hard work and caring.

To Marj Scariati and Keum Park, my caring, self-sacrificing intellectual property support team.

To Dr. Peter Green and Ann Roland Lee at Columbia University whose efforts and work on gluten intolerance have guided me.

And a heartfelt thanks to the many others who have cheered me on and supported me in this project.

TABLE OF CONTENTS

FOREWORD

CELIAC DISEASE IS MORE COMMON than most people realize. In fact, it affects about 1% of the population, or close to 3 million individuals, in the United States. But less than 3% of those with celiac disease are correctly diagnosed: the majority is unaware that they even have this condition. A result of this massive under-diagnosis is that Americans with celiac disease suffer from inadequate support systems. There is a lack of reliable food labeling, a lack of awareness in the food and grocery industry, inadequate knowledge among professional chefs, and a general lack of availability of gluten-free products. This is in marked contrast to the rest of the world!

At the Celiac Disease Center at Columbia University in New York City, we are educating health care professionals and facilitating a great variety of research projects with the goal of increasing the quality of patient care. It is through physician, dietitian, and nurse education that more people with celiac disease will be correctly diagnosed, and thus their lives improved.

We also know that good-tasting, gluten-free baked goods are difficult to find and very often expensive for individuals who need to maintain a gluten-free diet. But this wonderful book by Annalise Roberts helps fill the void. Chock full of accurate information and excellent recipes, it will help decrease the burden of the disease. It is a very readable book, and the recipes taste great!

Peter H. R. Green, M.D.
Anne R. Lee, R.D.
Celiac Disease Center at Columbia University, New York City
www.celiacdiseasecenter.columbia.edu

CHAPTER 1

What Are You Hungry For?

Well, and what then shall I tell you, my Lady, of the secrets of nature that I have learned while cooking? . . . One can philosophize quite well while preparing supper. I often say, when I make these little observations, "Had Aristotle cooked, he would have written a great deal more." —Sor Juana Ines de la Cruz[*]

WHEN I TEACH GLUTEN-FREE baking classes or advise newly diagnosed celiacs on how to cook, I always ask them what foods they miss most. In response, I always hear the same few answers: they miss the basics—bread, pizza, cake, pie, cookies. But I also hear the sheer longing in people's voices and the qualifying adjectives they feel compelled to include: *real* pizza, *really good* bread for sandwiches that tastes good and won't crumble, *real* crusty, chewy Italian or French bread, *really good* cake that's not dense and gritty, *really good* pie crust that doesn't taste like cardboard.

Perhaps you've said the same thing. Perhaps you're still hungry for the taste, the texture of something you once either took for granted or cherished every time you took a bite. If you *are* hungry for gluten-free recipes so good that no one will miss the wheat, read on.

For most of us, the search for a decent gluten-free recipe requires time, patience, compromise, and emotional strength. After my own diagnosis of celiac over three years ago, I thought I would never eat a really delicious piece of cake or a good hot, fresh muffin again. But I grew up baking, and I was determined to make gluten-free foods that were as wonderful as those I was used to. It became even more important when one of my sons was diagnosed with gluten intolerance.

The result is this collection of delicious, dependable gluten-free recipes for classic baked goods that look, feel, and taste as good as, or better than, their wheat-containing counterparts. They are all here, in this one book.

HOW OLD ARE YOUR MUFFINS?

Although gluten-free baked goods are available in natural food stores and online, they are usually frozen, often old tasting, and almost always shrink wrapped for "sell by" dates months in advance. But the worst part is that they are always expensive. This is especially true when

---

[*] *La respuesta / Sor Juana Ines de la Cruz.* Critical edition and translation by Electa Arenal and Amanda Powell. New York: Feminist Press at the City University of New York, 1994.

you are able to find them fresh. As more individuals are correctly diagnosed and more suppliers move into this potentially lucrative market, prices may come down. But for now, raw material prices, manufacturing constraints, and the incredibly poor distribution system combine to keep prices high.

Moreover, in order for mass production bakeries to make baked goods that stay fresh on the shelf as long as possible, they need to use more fat and sugar than you would use to make the same kind of baked goods at home. As distribution and pricing improve, gluten-free baked goods will no doubt fall prey to the fattening forces of even larger scale mass production. They will have even more added fat and sugar then they have now.

Time and effort aside, if you are going to eat and enjoy cake or muffins, you're better off making them yourself. They will be fresher, cost less, and have less fat and sugar than ones you buy at the store—wheat or no wheat.

BUT I DON'T HAVE TIME TO BAKE

I believe that what and how we eat affects our quality of life. Food can make us happier and healthier, and it is a manageable ingredient in our daily lives. Make the time to cook and bake. If you are too busy to cook, maybe you are just plain too busy. Noted social theorist Dr. Robin Fox wrote, "All animals eat, but we are the only animal that cooks. It is what makes us human."

For the gluten-intolerant, the need to cook without gluten cannot be ignored. Good take-out pizza is never a phone call away. But our gluten-free food should do more than simply nourish our bodies; it should also nurture our spirit. You cannot overestimate the happiness home-baked treats can bring to yourself and others. The carefully crafted recipes in this book will provide a foundation for a gluten-free baking repertoire that you can personalize and update for years to come.

CHAPTER 2

Gluten Reality

MANY OF OUR FAVORITE FOODS—a slice of pizza, a chocolate chip cookie, a flaky biscuit—were unknown to our ancestors. All of these delicious foods contain wheat, a grain not grown by man until relatively recently—about 7,000 years ago. You must consider that although *Homo sapiens* has been on the planet about 100,000 years, for 90,000 years the species ate only what it could find. This is the equivalent of a 45-year-old man adding wheat to his diet for the first time at about age 41.

Interestingly enough, today wheat has become part of a growing controversy about carbohydrates. Just how much bread, pasta, cake, and pizza can we eat without getting fat? Do these carbo-loaded foods make us sluggish? Are they good for our system? The questions are endless. Unfortunately, so are the answers. But one thing is sure: Wheat can make many of us sick. For people with celiac disease, the concerns are far more serious than whether or not wheat will make them fat.

Celiac is a genetic intolerance to gluten, a protein found in wheat, rye, and barley. When people with celiac disease eat foods containing gluten, their immune systems are triggered to attack the lining of their small intestine. This reaction causes inflammation and interferes with the digestion of vitamins, minerals, and other vital nutrients. Currently, the only effective treatment for celiac disease is a lifelong gluten-free diet.

Celiac is thought to be the most common genetic disease in Europe. It has also been identified in people from South America, the Near East, Pakistan, Cuba, and North Africa. Recent studies indicate that as many as 1 in 100 Americans of European descent may have the disease, although the actual diagnosis rate is 1 in 3,600. It is estimated that there are over 1 million people in the United States with undiagnosed celiac. In fact, it is the most misdiagnosed disease in America. Those with symptoms are often told they have other intestinal, digestive, emotional, or dermatologic problems, including irritable bowel syndrome, Crohn's disease, ulcerative colitis, diverticulosis, intestinal infections, arthritis, depression, and chronic fatigue syndrome.

Many doctors not only fail to correctly screen for celiac but they fail to consider it in the first place. The average time for an individual to be correctly diagnosed in the United States is over seven years.

Symptoms of celiac include diarrhea, constipation, bloating, stomach pain, skin rash, tooth enamel discoloration, joint and muscle pain, and many autoimmune syndromes (including rheumatoid arthritis, multiple sclerosis, lupus, psoriasis, thyroid disease, alopecia areata, and diabetes). Other associated conditions include: asthma, osteoporosis, iron deficiency anemia, short stature in children, female infertility, peripheral neuropathy, ADD, ADHD (and other learning problems), seizures and other neurologic syndromes, depression and other psychiatric syndromes. In addition, autism is emerging as a syndrome that may improve with a gluten-free diet.

WHY ARE SO MANY PEOPLE SENSITIVE TO GLUTEN?

Early man hunted for meat and fish and gathered fruits, seeds, herbs, tubers, and roots. As civilization progressed, crops of complex carbohydrates were cultivated for the purpose of stabilizing food supplies. Rice was the most cultivated species in Asia, sorghum and millet in Africa, and in America maize, or corn, was the major crop. Wheat and barley containing very low gluten content were grown only in Southwest Asia. As time went on, farming of wheat and barley spread into Europe. But our ancestors never ate bread as we know it today.

The industrial and agricultural revolutions of the past 200 years have changed our diet faster than we can change genetically. Today, our wheat crops have a high gluten content (50 percent higher than centuries ago in some cases) for the purpose of improved bread baking, and with it, we see a rise in the prevalence of gluten intolerance. Just as humans are predisposed to store excess calories as fat, the same genetic makeup that tolerated wheat with low gluten levels cannot tolerate modern foods with high gluten levels.

Unfortunately, we Americans have come to rely on wheat to fill our bellies. Instead of dining on the fruits, vegetables, meats, and fish eaten by our ancestors, today our diets are loaded with gluten-laden wheat-based foods: breads, pastas, pizza, cookies, muffins, and bagels. Gluten is also the second largest additive in all packaged foods (sugar is the largest). Its prevalence combined with an overall lack of knowledge about gluten intolerance means that the large number of individuals predicted to have celiac disease are not even aware that gluten could be the root cause of their ailments.

Modernization may have exacerbated gluten sensitivity, but luckily it provided gluten-free flour alternatives so that a child with celiac disease can enjoy a cupcake at his or her own birthday party. And now, for less money and in less time than it takes to go out and buy it, you can make a gluten-free dessert that's so delicious everyone will want some.

CHAPTER 3

Getting Started

CELIAC IS SERIOUS, but baking can be fun. It is part art and part science. It combines careful measurement with creative flavoring and decorating. My thoughts about gluten-free baking are in harmony with my basic philosophy about all cooking: It should be simple and not all-consuming. This chapter provides details on how to buy, mix, and measure gluten-free flours, discusses gluten-free baking know-how, and presents strategies for making time to bake in busy lives. I have much to tell you and secrets to share. So buy some xanthan gum and let's get baking!

WHAT CAN YOU EXPECT?

Chances are you didn't grow up watching your mother or grandmother bake gluten-free cookies. Even if you grew up baking, gluten-free flours change everything: how you measure ingredients; how much baking powder, baking soda, liquid, and eggs you use; baking time; and pan size. Although gluten-free baked goods are notoriously heavy and dense, they need not be. You can make gluten-free cakes and muffins that are as light as those made with wheat. You can make delicious cookies that are indistinguishable from their wheat-containing counterparts. You can make perfect pie and tart shells and New York pizza crusts so delicious you will never again feel pizza-deprived. But like all things worth achieving in life, you can expect that it might take a little time, thought, and energy.

The recipes in this book have been meticulously fine-tuned to produce excellent results—if you follow the directions. There are almost no shortcuts in baking; it is not like throwing a pasta dish together. Do not bother to try a new baking recipe unless you have the ingredients on hand, the equipment you need, and the time to concentrate and complete the task. I can't tell you how many times I've heard people tell me that a recipe failed and then admit that they substituted ingredients, didn't measure correctly, or were in a rush and probably left a step out.

Read each recipe completely before you actually begin to bake. Follow directions, measure all ingredients carefully, and check your oven temperature. Baking is the only form of cooking where a little bit too much or too little can ruin a recipe. Save your baking efforts for times when you are prepared. The result will be fabulous baked goods you, your family, and friends will happily consume.

HOW AND WHERE TO BUY GLUTEN-FREE FLOURS

All the baked goods in this book, *except the breads,* are made with one all-purpose Brown Rice Flour Mix. I use a combination of extra finely ground brown rice flour, potato starch (*not* potato flour), and tapioca flour (also called tapioca starch). Other gluten-free bakers provide a multitude of combinations, sometimes a different one for each recipe. Few people I know have large amounts of time to bake, much less to grab for four different flours each time they do. Fewer have room to store three or four different flour mixes in their cabinets. Following my philosophy that cooking should be simple, I want to be able to reach for one flour mix and know it will work dependably for almost everything I make.

The recipes in this book are carefully calibrated to work with the flour combination given below. Be aware that if you do in fact substitute flours, it will probably be necessary to adjust the amounts of other ingredients you use (most likely xanthan gum, liquids, and leavening agents). The recipe that follows gives you the formulas for mixing 3 cups and 9 cups of Brown Rice Flour Mix:

FOOD PHILOSOPHER™ GLUTEN-FREE
BROWN RICE FLOUR MIX

Brown rice flour (extra finely ground)	2 cups	6 cups
Potato starch *(not potato flour)*	⅔ cup	2 cups
Tapioca flour	⅓ cup	1 cup
Total	3 cups	9 cups

It is very important that you use an extra finely ground brown rice flour (not just any grind) or your baked goods will be gritty, heavy, and/or crumbly. Authentic Foods® in California (website, phone number, and address at end of chapter) sells just the right grind, as do many Asian grocery stores. Authentic Foods® rice flour is powdery, just like all-purpose wheat flour. Many other brands are not powdery, and it really does make a difference. If you use another rice flour, find one with the finest grind you can. It may be necessary to buy several different brands, open the packages, and feel the flour. Use the finest grinds for cakes, muffins, cookies, and pie crusts. Use the coarser grinds for pizza.

The potato starch (*not potato flour*) and tapioca flour (also called tapioca starch) can be found in local natural food stores, some grocery stores, and online. The brands seem fairly interchangeable and are consistent in quality.

In addition to the Brown Rice Flour Mix above, several cookie recipes, the buttermilk biscuits, and the Traditional Pie Crust recipe call for the inclusion of sweet rice flour. I use sweet rice flour to give these baked goods a better, less crumbly texture. It is available in local natural food stores, some grocery stores, and online. Again, I can recommend Authentic Foods® for their sweet rice flour, although the brand will not make a huge difference in your pie crust.

GLUTEN-FREE FLOURS FOR PIZZA

The pizza recipe in this book uses the Brown Rice Flour Mix but does not require finely ground brown rice flour and will actually have an improved texture with a coarser grind. Although I usually use my regular Brown Rice Flour Mix above, I will go out of my way to buy brown rice flour with a coarser grind when I know I'm going to bake a lot of pizza crusts for the freezer.

Bob's Red Mill® brown rice flour is great for pizza crust, and I am lucky enough to find it at my local grocery store. It can also be found in local natural food stores or ordered online. But there are many other brands of coarser ground brown rice flour, so you will no doubt be able to find one you like.

In addition to the Brown Rice Flour Mix, I use millet flour in pizza, although the recipe can be made without it (just substitute more of the brown rice flour). Millet is a delicious grain that improves the texture, taste, and nutritional content of some baked goods. I always use it whenever I make pizza. Arrowhead Mills® makes a good millet flour with consistent quality.

GLUTEN-FREE FLOURS FOR BREAD

If you are like me, you have baked and eaten more than your fair share of bad gluten-free bread. Over time, I developed recipes and three flour combinations for making breads that taste good, rise evenly without falling when they come out of the oven, and have the mouth feel and texture of some of the breads I missed most. All of my breads are made with a combination of millet, sorghum, cornstarch, potato starch (not potato flour), and tapioca flour (also called tapioca starch). Millet and sorghum are used to help vary the taste and improve nutrition. These flours produce bread with a wheat-like texture, compared to the gumminess of breads that contain rice flour.

The Submarine Sandwich Bread, French-Italian Bread, and Rustic Flat Bread (or Focaccia) use only Bread Flour Mix A. So you might want to mix a big batch. The Basic Sandwich Bread can be made with any of the three flour combinations below, although I like it best when made with Bread Flour Mix A. Bread Flour Mix A uses more millet than sorghum and has a very slight golden hue.

Bread Flour Mix B uses equal parts of millet and sorghum. It makes the lightest color bread and has the blandest taste. It is a good blend for newly gluten-intolerant children who are used to white bread. Both flour mixes make a sandwich bread that is much like homemade white bread in terms of texture and density.

Bread Flour Mix C uses garfava flour in addition to the millet, sorghum, cornstarch, potato starch, and tapioca flour. Garbanza beans and fava beans are used to make garfava flour. It is nutritious but has a stronger taste than most other gluten-free flours although that taste is tempered somewhat by the addition of the other flours. The bread it produces is delicious and perfect for sandwiches and toast. It is slightly lighter in texture than breads made with Bread Flour Mixes A and B.

However, many people, myself included, do not like the after-taste of the bean flour, which really comes through when you include it in bread used to make French toast, stuffing, or bread puddings. The breads made without any garfava flour will have a slightly heavier texture, but you will have a delicious, mild-tasting bread with none of the lingering bean flavor. Garfava flour is available in natural food stores, some grocery stores, and online.

FOOD PHILOSOPHER™ GLUTEN-FREE
BREAD FLOUR MIXES

Bread Flour Mix A

millet flour	2 cups	$^2/_3$ cup	$^1/_2$ cup
sorghum flour	1 cup	$^1/_3$ cup	$^1/_4$ cup
cornstarch	1 cup	$^1/_3$ cup	$^1/_4$ cup
potato starch	1 cup	$^1/_3$ cup	$^1/_4$ cup
tapioca flour	1 cup	$^1/_3$ cup	$^1/_4$ cup
Total	6 cups	2 cups	$1^1/_2$ cups

Bread Flour Mix B

millet flour	$1^1/_2$ cups	$^1/_2$ cup	$^1/_3$ cup plus 1 tablespoon
sorghum flour	$1^1/_2$ cups	$^1/_2$ cup	$^1/_3$ cup plus 1 tablespoon
cornstarch	1 cup	$^1/_3$ cup	$^1/_4$ cup
potato starch	1 cup	$^1/_3$ cup	$^1/_4$ cup
tapioca flour	1 cup	$^1/_3$ cup	$^1/_4$ cup
Total	6 cups	2 cups	$1^1/_2$ cups

Bread Flour Mix C

garfava bean flour	1 cup	$^1/_3$ cup	$^1/_4$ cup
sorghum flour	1 cup	$^1/_3$ cup	$^1/_4$ cup
millet flour	1 cup	$^1/_3$ cup	$^1/_4$ cup
cornstarch	1 cup	$^1/_3$ cup	$^1/_4$ cup
potato starch	1 cup	$^1/_3$ cup	$^1/_4$ cup
tapioca flour	1 cup	$^1/_3$ cup	$^1/_4$ cup
Total	6 cups	2 cups	$1^1/_2$ cups

HOW TO MEASURE AND MIX GLUTEN-FREE FLOURS

To measure flour for making flour mixes: Put the empty measuring cup into a small bowl. Use a soup spoon to spoon the flour from the package into the measuring cup, or pour the flour from the package into the measuring cup. Then use a knife or spoon handle to level the top (do this over the bowl to avoid a messy cleanup; pour the flour left in the bowl back into the package). *Do not scoop gluten-free flours* directly out of the package with the measuring cup.

As each flour is measured, transfer it into a plastic container large enough to leave four or five inches from the top unfilled. Shake container vigorously to mix flours. I usually make 12 cups of Brown Rice Flour Mix at a time and store and shake it in a 21-cup Rubbermaid® container.

To measure flour for use in recipes: *Shake* storage container vigorously to mix and aerate the flour mix. Put the empty measuring cup into a small bowl, or hold it over the opening of the container if it is large enough. Use soup spoon to spoon flour from the container into the measuring cup, then use a knife or spoon handle to level the top. If you do this over a bowl, pour the flour left in the bowl back into the storage container. *Do not scoop gluten-free flours* out of the storage container with the measuring cup. Remember: shake and bake!

THE ESSENTIAL NATURE OF GLUTEN-FREE FLOURS

You probably never thought about how much flavor wheat really has until you had to give it up. As a result, you may not realize that one of the things you actually miss most is the flavor of wheat. In my bread and pizza recipes, I try to compensate by using millet, a delicious, nutty-flavored grain, along with other more transparent flours like tapioca, cornstarch, and potato starch. In sweet baked goods, I try to mask the lack of wheat and cover up the brown rice flavor by accentuating the delicious flavors of other ingredients in the recipes. I use extra pure extracts and flavorings, more in fact, than a wheat recipe would call for.

The relative transparency of most of the gluten-free flours I use allows other flavors to shine through without affecting their taste. You will notice the essence of vanilla, lemon, almond, chocolate, and even butter in a whole new light. But remember, the relative tartness of yogurt or sour cream will also scream through with the same vibrant clarity.

THE SECRETS OF XANTHAN AND GUAR GUM

The gluten in wheat helps hold baked goods together and gives them elasticity. When we use gluten-free flours, we need to add back the elasticity by using xanthan gum and, sometimes, guar gum. These gums are water-soluble; technically they are called hydrocolloids. Because of their water-solubility, xanthan and guar gums improve mouth feel and build viscosity. They help retain moisture, provide elasticity, extend shelf life, encapsulate flavors, and stabilize baked goods so that they can be successfully frozen and thawed.

If you use too little xanthan or guar gum, your baked goods will fall apart and turn out brittle and hard. If you use too much, your baked goods will condense and shrink after you bake them, growing ever tighter and smaller as the gum works its magic for days after.

Xanthan gum is easy to find in natural food stores or online, is fairly consistent in quality across brands, and is very stable over a broad range of temperatures. I recommend it as the gum of choice for almost every recipe in the book. However, I recommend guar gum for my Angel Food Cake and the Vanilla and Chocolate Sponge Cakes. Guar gum increases in viscosity when heated and works really well in cakes without a lot of fat to help them stay tender.

HOW TO MEASURE INGREDIENTS FOR RECIPES IN THIS BOOK

Measure flour in nesting cups of 1, ½, ⅓, and ¼ cup capacity. Spoon ingredients into the measuring cup and level them off with the edge of a knife or the back of the spoon you used to transfer the ingredients. Measure other dry ingredients in measuring spoons the same way. Take care to be accurate. For instance, as much as ⅛ teaspoon too much xanthan gum will affect your baked goods! Measure liquids in glass or plastic measuring cups. Check at eye level.

INVEST IN GOOD QUALITY EQUIPMENT

I suggest you invest in good quality baking pans if you do not already have them. It will make a difference in your baked goods. Pans do not have to be professional quality. I use good, made-for-home bakeware that is readily available in stores everywhere, online, or in catalogs.

I use light-colored metal baking pans for recipe development, so if you have black metal pans, you will have to adjust the baking time. Food baked in black pans bakes faster because the dark surfaces absorb more of the radiant heat coming from the oven walls (as compared to pans with light, shiny surfaces which tend to reflect, rather than absorb, radiant energy). Therefore, baking times must be decreased for black pans.

I strongly recommend that you buy an instant-read thermometer because it will help you make good bread (as well as several other recipes in this book). You can buy them for under $5 at your grocery store. You do not need a fancy, expensive one.

HOW TO MELT CHOCOLATE FOR RECIPES IN THIS BOOK

The most commonly recommended method used to melt chocolate is in a double boiler. However, I find the quickest and easiest way is over direct heat, and although it demands more concentration and a heavy saucepan, it requires less time. Simply place coarsely chopped chocolate in a *heavy* saucepan over *low* heat. Stir constantly until melted. Immediately remove chocolate from heat to prevent scorching. Chocolate should never be heated beyond 120° to 125°F, and you should not add it to other ingredients until it cools down to about 105°F.

In addition, small amounts of chocolate can be melted in the microwave. Place coarsely chopped chocolate in a glass bowl. Microwave on medium/high for 1 to 1 ½ minutes for 1 to 3 ounces of chocolate. Stir every 30 seconds with a rubber spatula while melting. When melted, cover with plastic wrap until needed.

MAKING HALF THE RECIPE

Almost all of the recipes in this book can be cut in half. In fact, when I test recipes, I almost always make half a recipe first, so I know it can be done. Invest in measuring spoons that include a ⅛ teaspoon and measure carefully. Remember, a large egg is equal to 4 tablespoons (beat it well before measuring), and 1 tablespoon is equal to 3 teaspoons. You may want to write down the quantities for the recipe and cut them in half before you start (like I do) to avoid mistakes. You also may have to adjust baking times and pan sizes (sweet breads, for instance, can be baked in mini loaf pans).

STRATEGIES FOR MAKING TIME TO BAKE

- Prepare a batch of the Brown Rice Flour Mix whenever you run low so that you'll always have it available. If you have easy access to baking flour, you are more likely to bake whenever time is available or the urge strikes.

- Make sure you have what you need in your baking pantry to make the recipes you want (see pantry recommendations below).

- Make enough pizza crusts and cookie doughs to freeze and use over a month's time. I especially like to freeze cookie dough (each recipe includes freezing instructions), so that I can bake a small batch of fresh cookies every week without starting from scratch.

- Pre-measure and mix ingredients for breads you know you'll want to make in the course of a month *(do not add the yeast until you are ready to bake)*. You're more likely to make a loaf of bread if most of the steps have already been completed. There are two ways to do this: The way I recommend is to pre-measure and mix enough Bread Flour Mix to use for a month or more. Or you might consider mixing and storing all the dry ingredients needed for individual breads *(except the yeast)* in separate, clearly marked containers.

- I often try to pre-measure and mix dry ingredients for recipes ahead of time, so all I have to do is toss in the butter, eggs, and liquids when I am ready to bake. Sometimes I even pre-measure liquid ingredients and keep them covered (and refrigerated when necessary). I usually store pre-measured or pre-mixed dry ingredients in a tightly covered, labeled plastic container, but depending on what and when I plan on baking, I might just put them in a mixing bowl and cover it with plastic wrap. This is especially nice when I want to make fresh muffins or scones in the morning or serve fresh rustic flat bread or fruit crisp at dinner.

GLUTEN-FREE BAKING PANTRY

Non-Refrigerated

Extra-fine brown rice flour (recommended: Authentic Foods)*
Regular brown rice flour (optional for pizza)
Sweet rice flour (recommended: Authentic Foods)*
White rice flour (optional to dust baking pans)
Potato starch (not potato flour)
Tapioca flour (also called tapioca starch)
Cornstarch
Sorghum flour
Millet flour
Garfava bean flour

Xantham gum
Guar gum

Granulated sugar
Confectioner's sugar
Dark brown sugar
Light brown sugar

Dried buttermilk powder (keep refrigerated after opening)
Dried egg white powder
Molasses
Light corn syrup

Powdered cocoa
Semisweet chocolate morsels
Semisweet baking chocolate
Unsweetened baking chocolate
German sweet chocolate

Pure vanilla extract
Other pure extracts you use often: almond, lemon, etc.
Baking soda
Baking powder
Cream of tartar
Iodized salt
Sea salt
Mixed whole peppercorns and black ground pepper
A variety of dried herbs and spices including: allspice, basil, cardamom, cinnamon, ground cloves, crushed red pepper, dill weed, fennel seed, ground ginger, nutmeg, oregano, paprika, rosemary, sage, tarragon

White wine vinegar
White distilled vinegar or rice wine vinegar
Apple cider vinegar
Canola oil
Olive oil
Jars of your favorite pasta sauce or tomato sauce for pizza

Refrigerated
Butter and margarine
Heavy cream
Light cream
Eggs
Milk (I use fat-free for most recipes, but you can use 2% or whole)
Lemons (grated zest can be stored in freezer)
Prepared pesto (can be stored in freezer) for quiches, tarts, and pesto pizza
Bottled lemon juice
Bottled key lime juice
Assorted nuts for baking recipes, including walnuts, almonds, pecans

* Store open packages of brown rice flour in refrigerator. The Brown Rice Flour Mix does not need to be stored in refrigerator if you use it within three months.

THE LAST WORD ON BAKED GOODS

Baked goods are not the largest group recommended for consumption on the food pyramid, and they should not make up a significantly large part of your diet. Try to eat mostly fresh fruits, vegetables, meat, poultry, fish, beans, gluten-free whole grains like quinoa and buckwheat, and low-fat dairy products (but splurge on good cheese if you can!). However, when you do indulge in baked goods, they should be delicious, make you happy, and soothe your longing. Why waste the calories otherwise?

A recommended source for gluten-free flour:
Authentic Foods®
1860 W. 169th St., Suite B
Gardena, CA 90247
800-806-4737
www.authenticfoods.com

Muffins, Sweet Breads, and Scones

WARM FRAGRANT MUFFINS, sweet breads, and scones fresh from the oven can transform even the simplest breakfast or brunch into something very special. The recipes in this section were carefully developed to create delicious gluten-free baked goods you will be able to look forward to making and eating over and over.

Now, I didn't say they were fat-free, sugar-free nut-and-seed health muffins you can eat with utter abandon. No, these are the real thing. But remember that baked goods you make at home will typically have less fat and sugar than their store-bought counterparts (see Chapter 1). In fact, all the muffins and two of the sweet breads use canola oil rather than butter. Moreover, I used fat-free milk when I developed the recipes, so you can use the same (or low-fat milk) unless a recipe calls for a specific fat content.

On the other hand, I only use fresh eggs rather than egg substitutes. When a large egg is specified, it means that the fats in the yolk, as well as the whites, are needed to help ensure a sound structure and a good rise.

When you want to have fresh muffins or scones in the morning, I recommend you measure and combine the dry ingredients the night before (keep them tightly sealed). You can even pre-measure the liquids. Take out the pans so they will be on the counter when you need to prep them in the morning. Conversely, the sweet breads are best when they are made the day before because they are easier to slice when cold. Their flavor is best at room temperature.

This chapter uses the following pans:
- 12-inch muffin pan
- 9 x 5-inch loaf pan
- 8 ½ x 4 ½-inch loaf pan
- four 5 x 3-inch loaf pans
- 8-inch round cake pan
- Large, heavy baking sheet

THE LAST WORD ON MUFFINS
- Set-up before starting the recipe: assemble all ingredients
- Measure carefully (see Chapter 3)
- Use the right size pan
- Preheat the oven to the proper temperature (make sure oven is calibrated correctly)
- Do not open the oven door more than necessary
- Use a timer because you can get distracted

Once you mix the liquids into the dry ingredients, you need to get your muffins, sweet breads, or scones into the oven quickly. The baking powder leaps into action once it is combined with the liquid and creates the air pockets that will help your baked goods rise. So make sure your oven is preheated and your pans are prepared; it will make a difference in the texture and lightness of your baked goods.

Take note: The Blueberry and Apple Muffins are baked at 375°F rather than 350°F (most of the other muffins bake at 350°F). This is to compensate for the relatively cooler temperature and extra moisture of the fruit you add. You can bake them at 350°F, but the outsides will be softer and less firm.

CORNBREAD OR CORN MUFFINS

Makes 9 muffins or one 8-inch round bread

Cornbread is an American classic. One version or another can be found in every basic cookbook. I'd been making cornbread for decades and taking it for granted, that is, until I could no longer eat it. This is my favorite recipe—but with gluten-free flours. As a bread, this recipe is delicious on its own or with bowls of steamy chili. I also love to make it as corn muffins, served warm from the oven for breakfast with fresh creamy butter or fruit preserves. Either way, cornbread is one of those recipes you'll be happy to have in your repertoire.

> 1 cup cornmeal
>
> 1 cup Brown Rice Flour Mix (see p. 6)
>
> $\frac{1}{2}$ teaspoon xanthan gum
>
> $\frac{1}{4}$ cup granulated sugar
>
> $3\frac{1}{2}$ teaspoons baking powder
>
> $\frac{1}{4}$ teaspoon salt
>
> $\frac{1}{4}$ cup canola oil
>
> 1 cup milk minus 1 tablespoon
>
> 1 large egg, well beaten
>
> $\frac{1}{4}$ teaspoon pure vanilla extract

1. Preheat oven to 400°. Position rack in center of oven. Spray muffin pan or 8-inch round cake pan with cooking spray.

2. Mix dry ingredients in medium mixing bowl. Combine oil, milk, egg, and vanilla in another small bowl. Add wet ingredients to dry and gently stir to combine. Do not over mix. Pour batter into muffin pan or 8-inch round cake pan.

3. Bake about 20 minutes for muffins or about 25 minutes for bread. Remove from pan and serve immediately.

Muffins can be stored in a tightly sealed plastic container in refrigerator or covered with plastic wrap and then with foil and stored in freezer for up to three weeks. Best when eaten within four days of baking. Rewarm briefly in microwave.

BLUEBERRY MUFFINS

Makes 12 muffins

This is the first muffin recipe I converted to gluten-free because it had always been one of my favorites. The muffins are light and delicious and just like I remember them. Although the original recipe didn't include vanilla extract, I added it here to mask the brown rice flavor, which peeks through when the muffins are rewarmed in the microwave. Occasionally, I like to put on a Streusel Topping (recipe follows) because that is how my Mother made them for Sunday brunch.

My children weren't wild about blueberry muffins when they were small, so I made the same basic recipe for them but put in chocolate chips instead of blueberries. They were an instant hit. The recipe for Chocolate Chip Muffins, also converted from the original, is below.

Muffins can be stored in a tightly sealed plastic container in refrigerator or covered with plastic wrap and then with foil and stored in freezer for up to three weeks. Best when eaten within three days of baking. Rewarm briefly in a microwave.

* To make cinnamon sugar, combine 2 tablespoons sugar with $^1/_2$ teaspoon cinnamon.

   2 cups Brown Rice Flour Mix (see p. 6)
   $^2/_3$ cup granulated sugar
   1 tablespoon baking powder
   1 teaspoon baking soda
   $^3/_4$ teaspoon xanthan gum
   $^1/_4$ teaspoon salt
$^1/_4$–$^1/_2$ teaspoon nutmeg (to taste)
   $1^1/_2$ cups unsweetened fresh blueberries
   $^1/_2$ cup milk
   $^1/_2$ cup canola oil
   2 large eggs
   $^1/_2$ teaspoon pure vanilla extract
   Cinnamon sugar* for garnish *or* optional Streusel Topping, recipe follows

1. Preheat oven to 375°. Position rack in center of oven. Spray muffin pan with cooking spray.

2. Mix flour, sugar, baking powder, baking soda, xanthan gum, salt, and nutmeg in large mixing bowl. Add blueberries; stir to coat evenly.

3. Combine milk and oil in small bowl; remove 1 tablespoon of combined liquid and discard it. Beat in eggs and vanilla. Add liquids to blueberry mixture and stir until just blended.

4. Fill muffin pans $^2/_3$ full. Sprinkle top with cinnamon sugar or Streusel Topping (below). Bake 18–25 minutes until light golden. Remove muffins from pan and serve immediately or cool on a rack.

CHOCOLATE CHIP MUFFINS

Omit blueberries, nutmeg, and cinnamon sugar topping. Add 1 cup chocolate chips. Sprinkle top with granulated sugar or Streusel Topping. Bake at 350°F rather than 375°F.

STREUSEL TOPPING

$\frac{1}{2}$ cup Brown Rice Flour Mix (see p. 6)

$\frac{1}{3}$ cup brown sugar

$\frac{1}{2}$ teaspoon cinnamon

$\frac{1}{4}$ teaspoon xanthan gum

3 tablespoons unsalted butter, melted

1. Combine flour, brown sugar, cinnamon, and xanthan gum in a small bowl; stir to blend. Pour in butter and stir until all dry ingredients are moistened. Break into small pieces with spoon.

APPLE CINNAMON MUFFINS WITH STREUSEL TOPPING

Makes 12 muffins

I like to make these muffins in the fall and winter because a warm cinnamon-apple aroma floats out of the oven and fills the house. They require relatively little effort but give back a huge return in terms of making people happy. Even better, my family and friends still love them in their new gluten-free version. In the summer when fresh ripe peaches are available, you can make the same basic recipe using peaches and ground ginger instead of apples and cinnamon for another delicious breakfast treat.

2 cups Brown Rice Flour Mix (see p. 6)

²⁄₃ cup granulated sugar

1 tablespoon baking powder

1 teaspoon baking soda

³⁄₄ teaspoon xanthan gum

¹⁄₄ teaspoon salt

2 teaspoons cinnamon

1 cup peeled, chopped apple

¹⁄₂ cup chopped walnuts (optional)

¹⁄₂ cup milk

¹⁄₂ cup canola oil

2 large eggs

Streusel Topping (recipe follows) *or* cinnamon sugar* for garnish

Muffins can be stored in a tightly sealed plastic container in refrigerator or covered with plastic wrap and then with foil and stored in freezer for up to three weeks. Best when eaten within three days of baking. Rewarm briefly in microwave.

* To make cinnamon sugar, combine 2 tablespoons granu-lated sugar with ¹⁄₂ teaspoon cinnamon.

1. Preheat oven to 375°. Position rack in center of oven. Spray muffin pan with cooking spray.

2. Mix flour, sugar, baking powder, baking soda, xanthan gum, salt, and cinnamon in large mixing bowl. Add apples and walnuts; stir to coat evenly.

3. Combine milk and oil in small bowl; remove 1 tablespoon of combined liquid and discard it. Beat in eggs. Add liquids to apple mixture and stir until just blended.

4. Fill muffin pans ²⁄₃ full. Top with streusel. Bake 18–25 minutes until light golden. Remove from pan and serve immediately or cool on a rack.

PEACH GINGER MUFFINS

Omit apples, walnuts, and cinnamon. Add 2 cups peeled and chopped fresh peaches, $\frac{1}{2}$ teaspoon pure vanilla extract, $\frac{1}{2}$ teaspoon (or to taste) ground ginger. Sprinkle muffin tops with granulated sugar.

STREUSEL TOPPING

$\frac{1}{2}$ cup Brown Rice Flour Mix (see p. 6)

$\frac{1}{3}$ cup brown sugar

$\frac{1}{2}$ teaspoon cinnamon

$\frac{1}{4}$ teaspoon xanthan gum

3 tablespoons unsalted butter, melted

1. Combine flour, brown sugar, cinnamon, and xanthan gum in a small bowl; stir to blend. Pour in butter and stir until all dry ingredients are moistened. Break into small pieces with spoon.

Peach muffins do not keep well because fresh peaches are so wet they can make the muffins a bit soggy. They are best when eaten within two days of baking. Try making half the recipe if you won't be able to eat them within this time frame.

LEMON COCONUT MUFFINS

Makes 12 muffins

Years ago, I used to love going through the Union Square Green Market in New York City on my way to work. One of my favorite stands was The Muffin Man who offered up a table of delicious fresh muffins. My absolute favorite was his lemon coconut muffin. When I stopped working in the City, I searched all over to find one as good as his, to no avail. So I made them myself.

Fragrant with lemon and coconut, delicate yet with more body than a blueberry muffin, I still crave them. Fortunately, I was able to satisfy that craving with this true to the original gluten-free version. Take note that the natural acidity in the lemon works with xanthan gum to tighten the muffin a bit more than muffins without lemon. They will be slightly smaller after the first day or if you freeze them.

Muffins can be stored in a tightly sealed plastic container in refrigerator or covered with plastic wrap and then with foil and stored in freezer for up to three weeks. Best when eaten within three days of baking. Rewarm briefly in microwave.

2 cups Brown Rice Flour Mix (see p. 6)

$\frac{2}{3}$ cup granulated sugar

1 tablespoon baking powder

1 teaspoon baking soda

$\frac{3}{4}$ teaspoon xanthan gum

$\frac{1}{4}$ teaspoon salt

1 cup sweetened flaked coconut

1 packed tablespoon grated lemon rind

$\frac{1}{2}$ cup milk

$\frac{1}{2}$ cup canola oil

2 large eggs

1. Preheat oven to 350°. Position rack in center of oven. Spray muffin pan with cooking spray.

2. Mix flour, sugar, baking powder, baking soda, xanthan gum, and salt in large mixing bowl. Add coconut and lemon rind and stir to combine.

3. Combine milk and oil in small bowl; remove 1 tablespoon of combined liquid and discard it. Beat in eggs. Add liquids to flour mixture and stir until just blended.

4. Fill muffin pans $\frac{2}{3}$ full. Sprinkle top with granulated sugar. Bake 18–25 minutes until light golden. Remove from pan and serve immediately.

LEMON POPPY SEED MUFFINS

Omit coconut. Add $\frac{1}{4}$ cup poppy seeds and 2 packed tablespoons grated lemon rind. Sprinkle top with granulated sugar.

CHOCOLATE RICOTTA MUFFINS

Makes 10 muffins

These muffins are so good you won't be able to keep people from eating the entire batch after you take them from the oven. They are excellent for an afternoon snack or a with a cup of coffee in the late morning. They have a rich chocolate flavor and a tender texture. Although I always make them with fat-free milk and low-fat ricotta cheese, you could use a higher-fat milk and whole-milk ricotta and they would still be delicious.

1¼ cups Brown Rice Flour Mix (see p. 6)

¼ cup unsweetened cocoa powder

½ cup granulated sugar

1½ teaspoons baking powder

½ teaspoon baking soda

¼ teaspoon xanthan gum

¼ teaspoon salt

⅔ cup semisweet chocolate chips

1 large egg

½ cup ricotta cheese (part skim)

⅔ cup milk

2 tablespoons canola oil

2 teaspoons pure vanilla extract

1. Preheat oven to 350°F. Position rack in center of oven. Spray muffin pan with cooking spray or line with paper baking cup liners.

2. Whisk flour, cocoa, sugar, baking powder, baking soda, xanthan gum, and salt together in a large mixing bowl. Stir in chocolate chips.

3. In another medium mixing bowl whisk egg, ricotta, milk, oil, and vanilla together until well blended.

4. Pour the milk mixture into the flour mixture and combine until well blended. Do not over beat.

5. Spoon batter into prepared muffin cups and place in center of oven. Bake for 18–20 minutes until toothpick inserted in center of a muffin comes out clean. Remove from pan and serve immediately or cool on a rack.

Muffins can be stored in a tightly sealed plastic container in refrigerator or covered with plastic wrap and then with foil and stored in freezer for up to three weeks. Best when eaten within four days of baking. Rewarm briefly in microwave.

CARROT SPICE MUFFINS

Makes 12 muffins

I have to admit I only started making these muffins recently, but they have become a favorite in my household. The delicate flavor of carrot combined with crunchy walnuts, sweet coconut, cinnamon, and nutmeg can really brighten up a morning. If you like carrot cake, you will undoubtedly enjoy eating these muffins. The only problem will be trying not to eat too many.

2 cups Brown Rice Flour Mix (see p. 6)

$^2/_3$ cup granulated sugar

1 tablespoon baking powder

1 teaspoon baking soda

$^3/_4$ teaspoon xanthan gum

2 teaspoons cinnamon

$^1/_2$ teaspoon nutmeg

$^1/_4$ teaspoon salt

1 cup finely shredded carrot

$^1/_2$ cup finely chopped walnuts

$^1/_2$ cup sweetened shredded coconut

$^1/_2$ cup milk

$^1/_2$ cup canola oil

2 large eggs

1 teaspoon pure vanilla extract

Cinnamon sugar* for garnish

Muffins can be stored in a tightly sealed plastic container in refrigerator or covered with plastic wrap and then with foil and stored in freezer for up to three weeks. Best when eaten within four days of baking. Rewarm briefly in microwave.

* To make cinnamon sugar, combine 2 tablespoons sugar with $^1/_2$ teaspoon cinnamon.

1. Preheat oven to 350°. Position rack in center of oven. Spray muffin pan with cooking spray.

2. Mix flour, sugar, baking powder, baking soda, xanthan gum, cinnamon, nutmeg, and salt in large mixing bowl. Add carrots, walnuts, and coconut; stir to coat evenly.

3. Combine milk and oil in small bowl; remove 1 tablespoon of combined liquid and discard it. Beat in eggs and vanilla. Add liquids to flour mixture and stir until just blended.

4. Fill muffin pans $^2/_3$ full. Sprinkle top with cinnamon sugar. Bake 18–25 minutes until light golden. Remove from pan and serve immediately or cool on a rack.

CRANBERRY NUT BREAD

It wouldn't be Thanksgiving in my home without this bread. I make it in the traditional way, flavored with sweet orange and crunchy walnuts. My Mother served the original version every year, and it was the first sweet bread I tried to convert from my recipe box. The first year that I was brave enough to serve it at Thanksgiving in its new gluten-free version I didn't say a word to anyone. Eventually, my Mother noticed me eating a piece and asked me if I would get sick from the wheat. I knew then that I could stop testing the recipe.

2 cups Brown Rice Flour Mix (see p. 6)

1 cup granulated sugar

2 teaspoons baking powder

¾ teaspoon xanthan gum

¾ teaspoon salt

½ teaspoon baking soda

¼ cup shortening

⅔ cup fresh orange juice

1 large egg, slightly beaten

2 cups fresh cranberries, coarsely chopped

½ cup shelled walnuts, coarsely chopped

1 tablespoon freshly grated orange rind

Granulated sugar (optional)

1. Preheat oven to 350°F. Position rack in center of oven. Spray 9 x 5-inch loaf pan or three 5 x 3-inch loaf pans with cooking spray.

2. Mix flour, sugar, baking powder, xanthan gum, salt, and baking soda in large bowl of electric mixer.

3. Blend in shortening until mixture resembles fine cornmeal. Pour in orange juice and egg and mix just until moistened. Fold in cranberries, walnuts, and orange rind.

4. Pour batter into prepared pan, sprinkle with granulated sugar (optional), and place in center of oven. Bake about 1 hour for 9 x 5-inch loaf or 45 minutes for 5 x 3-inch loaves (until knife inserted in center comes out clean.)

5. Cool bread for 10 minutes and then remove from pan. Cool completely on rack before serving or wrapping for storage. Easiest to slice when chilled.

Makes one 9 x 5-inch loaf or three 5 x 3-inch loaves

Store bread covered tightly with plastic wrap in refrigerator for up to five days. Can be covered with plastic wrap and then with foil and stored in freezer for up to six weeks. Best when eaten within four days of baking.

PUMPKIN BREAD OR MUFFINS

Makes 12 muffins or three 5 x 3-inch loaves

I like to make Pumpkin Bread in the autumn when the fall colors are peeking through my window. It seems so perfect for morning coffee or afternoon snacks once the weather starts to get cool. Your home will be filled with the warm aroma of sweet cinnamon, ginger, nutmeg, and cloves. This recipe makes traditionally moist, tender mini-loaves or muffins. Both freeze well, so you can make some for the holidays several weeks ahead.

$1\frac{3}{4}$ cups Brown Rice Flour Mix (see p. 6)

  1 cup granulated sugar

  1 teaspoon baking soda

  $\frac{3}{4}$ teaspoon xanthan gum

  $\frac{3}{4}$ teaspoon salt

  $\frac{1}{2}$ teaspoon baking powder

  $\frac{1}{2}$ teaspoon cinnamon

  $\frac{1}{2}$ teaspoon nutmeg

  $\frac{1}{2}$ teaspoon ground ginger

  $\frac{1}{4}$ teaspoon ground cloves

  2 large eggs

  $\frac{1}{4}$ cup water

  $\frac{1}{3}$ cup plus 2 tablespoons canola oil

  2 tablespoons molasses

  1 cup pumpkin puree

1. Preheat oven to 350°F. Position rack in center of oven. Spray three 5 x 3-inch loaf pans or muffin pan with cooking spray.

2. Mix flour, sugar, baking soda, xanthan gum, salt, baking powder, cinnamon, nutmeg, ginger, and cloves together in large mixing bowl of electric mixer.

3. Combine eggs, water, oil, molasses, and pumpkin in a separate bowl. Whisk to blend.

4. Pour the wet ingredients into dry and mix until well blended. Do not over beat.

5. Pour batter evenly into pans and bake 45–55 minutes for loaves and about 20–25 minutes for muffins or until toothpick inserted in center comes out clean.

6. Cool loaves for 8 minutes and then remove from pans. Remove muffins from pan immediately. Cool completely on rack before serving or wrapping for storage. Easiest to slice when chilled.

Store bread covered tightly with plastic wrap in refrigerator for up to five days. Muffins can be stored in a tightly sealed plastic container. Pumpkin Bread or Muffins can be covered with plastic wrap and then with foil and stored in freezer for up to six weeks. Best when eaten within four days of baking.

TRIPLE GINGER TEA LOAF

I first tasted this tender tea bread more than ten years ago when a friend brought me one for Christmas. I've been making it ever since and serving it throughout the holidays. It features a delicious blend of crystallized, fresh, and ground ginger in a fragrant loaf sweetened with light brown sugar. The bread slices more easily when chilled, so make it at least one day before you want to serve it. In fact, my gluten-free version of Triple Ginger Tea Loaf can be made well in advance (follow storage instructions below) because it stores well.

Makes one 8 ½ x 4 ½-inch loaf or three 5 x 3-inch loaves

1⅔ cups Brown Rice Flour Mix (see p. 6)

2 tablespoons buttermilk powder

1½ teaspoons baking soda

½ teaspoon xanthan gum

1 teaspoon ground ginger

1 teaspoon ground cinnamon

½ teaspoon ground cardamom

½ teaspoon salt

6 tablespoons minced crystallized ginger (about 2 ounces), divided

½ cup unsalted butter, room temperature

½ cup granulated sugar

½ cup golden light brown sugar

2 large eggs

2 tablespoons grated peeled fresh ginger

½ cup water

1. Preheat oven to 350°F. Position rack in center of oven. Spray 8 ½ x 4 ½-inch loaf pan or three 5 x 3-inch loaf pans with cooking spray.

2. Mix flour, buttermilk powder, baking soda, xanthan gum, ground ginger, cinnamon, cardamom, salt, and 3 tablespoons crystallized ginger in medium bowl. Set aside.

3. Beat butter and both sugars in large bowl of electric mixer until light and fluffy. Beat in eggs one at a time. Mix in grated fresh ginger. Add flour mixture and water and mix just until blended.

4. Pour batter into prepared pans and sprinkle top with remaining 3 tablespoons minced crystallized ginger. Press ginger lightly into batter. Place in center of oven and bake 35–40 minutes for small

loaves or until knife inserted in center comes out clean. Bake 50 minutes for large loaf; if necessary, turn oven to 250°F and bake another 5–10 minutes until knife inserted in center comes out clean.

5. Cool bread for 8 minutes and then remove from pans. Cool completely on rack before serving or wrapping for storage. Easiest to slice when chilled.

LEMON POPPY SEED TEA LOAVES

*Makes four
5 x 3-inch loaves*

These are the kind of delicate little lemon breads you're served with your morning meal at old-fashioned bed and breakfasts. Light, bursting with lemon flavor and crunchy poppy seeds, they are one of life's pleasures. Bake up a batch to serve for a Sunday brunch or afternoon tea. In their new gluten-free form they stay fresh for days in the refrigerator and freeze so well that you'll be able to enjoy them several weeks later.

> 2 cups Brown Rice Flour Mix (see p. 6)
> 2 teaspoons baking powder
> ¾ teaspoon xanthan gum
> ½ teaspoon salt
> ¼ cup poppy seeds
> 2 packed tablespoons grated lemon rind
> 1 cup granulated sugar
> ½ cup canola oil
> 3 large eggs
> ½ teaspoon lemon extract
> ¾ cup milk
> Granulated sugar

Store breads covered tightly with plastic wrap in refrigerator for up to five days. Breads can be covered with plastic wrap and then with foil and stored in freezer for up to six weeks. Best when eaten within four days of baking.

1. Preheat oven to 350°. Position rack in center of oven. Spray four 5 x 3-inch loaf pans with cooking spray.

2. Mix flour, baking powder, xanthan gum, salt, poppy seeds, and lemon rind in medium mixing bowl. Set aside.

3. Combine sugar, oil, eggs, and lemon extract in large bowl of electric mixer. Beat for 1 minute at medium-high speed. Add flour mixture and milk and mix until just blended.

4. Fill loaf pans with batter. Sprinkle tops with granulated sugar. Bake 35–40 minutes or until toothpick inserted in center comes out clean.

5. Cool breads for 10 minutes and then remove from pans. Cool completely on rack before serving or wrapping for storage. Easiest to slice when chilled.

LEMON WALNUT TEA LOAVES

Omit poppy seeds. Add ¾ cup finely chopped walnuts.

ORANGE JUICE BREAD

*Makes one
9 x 5-inch loaf*

I have been making this bread for longer than I can remember, and it never fails to surprise me how delicate and fragrant it is. The essence of sweet orange fills the kitchen when it's baking, and then the loaf stays fresh and flavorful for days after, even in its new gluten-free form. This tender bread makes a delicious treat for cold winter mornings with your last cup of coffee or as a special accompaniment to a cup of afternoon tea.

Store bread covered tightly with plastic wrap in refrigerator for up to five days. Can be covered with plastic wrap and then with foil and stored in freezer for up to six weeks. Best when eaten within four days of baking.

$1\frac{1}{2}$ cups Brown Rice Flour Mix (see p. 6)

$1\frac{1}{2}$ teaspoons baking powder

$\frac{1}{2}$ teaspoon xanthan gum

$\frac{1}{4}$ teaspoon salt

Grated rind from 1 large orange

1 tablespoon grated lemon rind

$\frac{1}{2}$ cup unsalted butter, room temperature

1 cup granulated sugar

2 large eggs

$\frac{1}{2}$ cup fresh orange juice

$\frac{1}{4}$ teaspoon lemon extract

Granulated sugar

1. Preheat oven to 350°F. Position rack in center of oven. Spray 9 x 5-inch loaf pan with cooking spray.

2. Mix flour, baking powder, xanthan gum, salt, and orange and lemon rind in medium bowl. Set aside.

3. Beat butter and sugar in large bowl of electric mixer until light and fluffy. Beat in eggs one at a time. Add flour mixture, orange juice, and lemon extract and mix just until blended.

4. Pour batter into prepared pan and sprinkle top with granulated sugar. Place pan in center of oven and bake for 45 minutes or until knife inserted in center comes out clean.

5. Cool bread for 10 minutes and then remove from pan. Cool completely on rack before serving or wrapping for storage. Easiest to slice when chilled.

ORANGE JUICE PECAN BREAD

Add $\frac{3}{4}$ cup chopped pecans.

TRADITIONAL SCONES

Scones have become popular in this country, although most American versions tends to be sweeter and heavier than their traditional English relatives. The best traditional scones I've had on this side of the Atlantic were in a New York City restaurant called Sarabeth's Kitchen. When I saw her recipe in a magazine many years ago, I cut it out and it became a favorite in my household.

After repeated attempts to recreate it in a gluten-free form, I came up with this recipe for a delicious traditional-style scone that soothed my longing. The trick is to make sure you really beat the eggs until they are very light and foamy. Just follow the directions carefully—no shortcuts—and you'll have a scone you could proudly serve at an English high tea.

$\frac{1}{2}$ cup milk

$\frac{1}{2}$ cup raisins

2 cups Brown Rice Flour Mix (see p. 6)

1 tablespoon granulated sugar

1 tablespoon baking powder

$\frac{3}{4}$ teaspoon xanthan gum

$\frac{1}{2}$ teaspoon salt

5 tablespoons butter, cut into small pieces

2 large eggs

1. Preheat oven to 425°F. Position rack in center of oven. Line heavy baking sheet with parchment paper.

2. Combine milk and raisins in glass measuring cup and set aside.

3. Combine flour, sugar, baking powder, xanthan gum, and salt in large bowl of electric mixer. With mixer on low, cut butter into flour mixture until it resembles a course meal. Put mixture into a small bowl and set aside.

4. Beat eggs in the same large bowl of electric mixer until *very light and foamy*. Add milk and flour mixtures all at once, and mix at medium-low speed for 1 minute. Use lightly floured hands to pat out dough into a large, 1-inch-thick round on lightly floured surface. Cut out scones with a $2\frac{1}{2}$-inch round cookie cutter. Press dough scraps together and repeat.

5. Place dough on prepared baking sheet and put in center of oven. Turn oven temperature down to 375°F and bake 20 to 25 minutes until golden and cooked through. Serve warm with butter or preserves.

Makes 9–10 scones

Store leftover scones in an airtight container in refrigerator. Or cover scones with plastic wrap and then with foil and store in freezer for up to three weeks. Best when eaten within four days of baking. Rewarm in a preheated 350°F oven for 5 to 10 minutes. Do not use a microwave!

LEMON CORNMEAL SCONES

Makes 14 scones

These fragrant, crunchy scones are bursting with lemon flavor. Traditional in shape and not too sweet, they're perfect for breakfast or afternoon tea with jam or preserves. Make sure you really beat the eggs until they are very light and foamy, and follow the directions carefully. These scones keep well in the refrigerator for several days and reheat easily in a preheated oven (do not use a microwave!). They are sure to become a favorite you'll make often.

$\frac{1}{2}$ cup milk

1 cup golden raisins

$1\frac{3}{4}$ cups Brown Rice Flour Mix (see p. 6)

1 cup stone-ground yellow cornmeal

$\frac{1}{4}$ cup granulated sugar

4 teaspoons baking powder

$\frac{3}{4}$ teaspoon xanthan gum

$\frac{1}{2}$ teaspoon salt

6 tablespoons butter, cut into small pieces

2 large eggs

1 teaspoon grated lemon rind

2 teaspoons pure vanilla extract

$\frac{1}{2}$ teaspoon pure lemon extract

Store leftover scones in an airtight container in refrigerator. Or cover them with plastic wrap and then with foil and store in freezer for up to three weeks. Best when eaten within four days of baking. Rewarm in a pre-heated 350°F oven for 5 to 10 minutes.

1. Preheat oven to 425°F. Position rack in center of oven. Line heavy baking sheet with parchment paper.

2. Combine milk and raisins in glass measuring cup and set aside.

3. Combine flour, cornmeal, sugar, baking powder, xanthan gum, and salt in large bowl of electric mixer. With mixer on low, cut butter into flour mixture until it resembles a course meal. Put mixture into a small bowl and set aside.

4. Beat eggs in the same large bowl of electric mixer until *very light and foamy*. Add milk and flour mixtures, grated lemon rind, and vanilla and lemon extracts all at once and mix at medium-low speed for 1 minute. Use lightly floured hands to pat out dough into a large, 1-inch-thick round on lightly floured surface. Cut out scones with a 2$\frac{1}{2}$-inch round cookie cutter. Press dough scraps together and repeat.

5. Place dough on prepared baking sheet and put in center of oven. Turn oven temperature down to 375°F and bake 20–25 minutes until golden and cooked through. Serve warm with jam or preserves.

CHAPTER 5

Cakes

WE ARE LUCKY. Cake comes in so many shapes, sizes, textures, and flavors that we are sure to have a favorite no matter how particular we are. The trick is converting that favorite to gluten-free. I found after much trial and error that there are, indeed, tricks to making a great gluten-free cake. Some are common sense and basic, others will start to make sense once you understand the nature of the ingredients.

Since gluten-free flours tend to be heavier and grainier than wheat, it really is important to use finely ground brown rice flour for cake. Because the flours can produce a denser crumb, we often use canola oil instead of butter with great results (and we often use slightly less fat in general). We typically use less liquid and a little more leavening. We have to adjust flavors: reduce salt because it will stand out and increase vanilla or other extracts to cover up the lack of wheat. We also use the smallest pan possible to get a good rise because no matter how hard you try, it will be difficult to get a round 12-inch or a 9 x 12-inch gluten-free cake to rise correctly.

There are a wide variety of cakes in this chapter. Some are so simple, like Vanilla Cupcakes and Chocolate Chip Pound Cake, that you might make them all the time. Others, such as the Angel Food Cake, might seem more complicated. But if you follow the directions, you will be

YELLOW LAYER CAKE

VANILLA CUPCAKES

VANILLA (BUTTER) LAYER CAKE

LEMON LAYER CAKE

MAPLE WALNUT CAKE

COCONUT LAYER CAKE

CHOCOLATE FUDGE CAKE

GERMAN CHOCOLATE CAKE

FLOURLESS CHOCOLATE CAKE

ANGEL FOOD CAKE

VANILLA SPONGE CAKE or
JELLY ROLL

CHOCOLATE SPONGE CAKE or
JELLY ROLL

CARROT CAKE

GINGERBREAD

NEW YORK CHEESECAKE

CLASSIC CHEESECAKE

CUSTARD CAKE WITH FRUIT
Custard Cake with Cherries

SOUR CREAM COFFEE CAKE

VANILLA POUND CAKE
Chocolate Chip Pound Cake

LEMON POUND CAKE
Lemon Blueberry Pound Cake
Lemon Poppy Seed Pound Cake

able to make a fabulous cake that you'll be delighted to serve. If you are new to baking cakes from scratch, start with the Vanilla Cupcakes or Yellow Layer Cake. They are so easy that I use them in my Introduction to Gluten-Free Baking class. With one success under your apron, branch out and try some of the others until you can make all your favorites.

This chapter uses the following pans:
- 8-inch round cake pan
- 9-inch round cake pan
- 12-muffin pan
- 9-inch (across the top) kugelhoph crown-shaped mold, or a fluted ring mold that holds 8 to 10 cups filled to the top rim (it is also called a small bundt pan with 4- to 6-cup capacity)
- 9-inch flat-bottom tube pan with removable bottom
- 9-inch round springform pan
- 10-inch springform pan
- Three 5 x 3-inch loaf pans
- Glass (Pyrex) or ceramic deep-dish pie pan (for custard cake)

THE LAST WORD ON CAKES
- Set-up before starting the recipe: assemble all the ingredients
- Separate eggs when they are cold, then let them warm to room temperature
- Measure carefully (see Chapter 3)
- *Follow the directions carefully.* When it says beat the eggs until foamy before adding sugar, or add sugar to the eggs (or butter) a little at a time, or beat eggs until thick and lemon colored, or beat butter until light and fluffy—please do it, as there is a reason
- Use the right size pan
- Preheat the oven to the proper temperature (make sure the oven is calibrated correctly)
- Do not open the oven door more than necessary
- Use a timer because you can get distracted
- Once you mix the liquids into the dry ingredients, you need to get your cakes into the oven fairly quickly. The baking powder leaps into action once it is combined with the liquid and creates the air pockets that will help your baked goods to rise. So make sure your oven is pre-heated and your pans are prepared; it will make a difference in the texture and lightness of your baked goods

YELLOW LAYER CAKE

One way to tell the quality of a baker is by how good their most basic cake is—not the icing mind you, just the cake by itself. The texture, taste, and appearance of this cake will please and delight you if you've been looking for a great yellow cake. It is versatile and can be used with light whipped frostings as well as denser buttercreams and chocolate ganache. It holds up well in the refrigerator and can also be frozen for up to three weeks. You will find this basic yellow cake a welcome addition to your gluten-free baking repertoire.

2 cups granulated sugar

4 large eggs

2½ cups Brown Rice Flour Mix (see p. 6)

½ teaspoon salt

1 tablespoon baking powder

1 teaspoon xanthan gum

1 cup canola oil

1 cup milk

2 teaspoons pure vanilla extract

2 cups of your favorite frosting

1. Preheat oven to 350°F. Position rack in center of oven. Line 2 round 9-inch layer cake pans with parchment or waxed paper and spray with cooking spray.

2. Beat sugar and eggs in large bowl of electric mixer at medium speed for 1 minute. Add flour, salt, baking powder, xanthan gum, oil, milk, and vanilla; beat at medium speed for 1 minute.

3. Pour batter into prepared pans. Place in center of oven and bake about 35 minutes (40 minutes for an 8-inch cake, 18–20 minutes for cupcakes) or until center springs back when touched and cake has pulled away from sides of pan.

4. Cool cake layers in the pans on a rack for 5 minutes. Use a small knife to cut around pan sides to loosen cake. Invert cake layers onto a rack, peel off parchment, and cool completely.

5. Place one cake layer on a platter. Spread 1 cup of frosting over top and sides. Place second layer on top. Spread remaining frosting over entire cake.

Makes two 8- or 9-inch rounds or 24 cupcakes

Serve slightly chilled or at room temperature. Can be made a day ahead. Store frosted cake in refrigerator. Unfrosted cake layers can be covered tightly with plastic wrap and stored in refrigerator for one day. Unfrosted cake layers can also be covered with plastic wrap and then with foil and stored in freezer for up to three weeks. Best when eaten within 3 three days of baking.

To make a four-layer cake: chill unfrosted layers until very cold or freeze briefly. Slice horizontally across each layer.

VANILLA CUPCAKES

*Makes 12 cupcakes or
one 8- or 9-inch round*

These vanilla cupcakes are delicious and easy to make; they literally take minutes to prepare. Once you try them, you'll think twice about using a cake mix ever again. The recipe is actually the Yellow Layer Cake (preceding recipe) cut in half because that is how I came to use it the most: for a small, quick batch of cupcakes. The texture of the cake is light and flavorful, with a tender crumb. Use your favorite frostings, or create mini-shortcakes with fresh fruit and whipped cream. But no matter how you make them, these cupcakes are sure to become a favorite in your home.

*Serve slightly chilled or
at room temperature.
Can be made a day
ahead. Store frosted
cupcakes in refrigerator.
Unfrosted cupcakes
can be covered tightly
with plastic wrap and
stored in refrigerator
for one day. Unfrosted
cupcakes can also be
covered with plastic
wrap and then with
foil and stored in
freezer for up to three
weeks. Best when
eaten within three
days of baking.*

1 cup granulated sugar

2 large eggs

1¼ cups Brown Rice Flour Mix (see p. 6)

¼ teaspoon salt

1½ teaspoons baking powder

½ teaspoon xanthan gum

½ cup canola oil

½ cup milk

1 teaspoon pure vanilla extract

Prepared frosting

1. Preheat oven to 350°F. Position rack in center of oven. Place cupcake baking liners in a 12-cupcake baking pan.

2. Beat sugar and eggs in large bowl of electric mixer at medium speed for 1 minute. Add flour, salt, baking powder, xanthan gum, oil, milk, and vanilla; beat at medium speed for 1 minute.

3. Pour batter into prepared pan. Place in center of oven and bake for about 20 minutes or until center springs back when touched and cupcakes are very lightly browned (bake about 35 minutes for 9-inch round, 40 minutes for 8-inch round).

4. Cool on rack for 5 minutes. Remove cupcakes from pan onto rack and cool completely before icing.

5. Top with your favorite frosting.

VANILLA (BUTTER) LAYER CAKE

Makes two 8- or 9-inch rounds. Recipe can be cut in half

I originally created this cake for a woman who wanted a gluten-free white wedding cake. She was looking for the slightly firmer consistency of cakes used to make the tiered pastry extravaganzas we associate with those festive occasions. The original version used separated eggs, but I found I was able to skip that step and still make a great cake that rose well, had a fine texture, and tasted delicious. Unlike white cakes made with wheat, the egg yolks are needed to give structure, so this cake will not really be white in the purest sense. But it is so good no one will even notice.

1½ cups granulated sugar

½ cup unsalted butter (at room temperature)

4 large eggs (at room temperature)

2 cups Brown Rice Flour Mix (see p. 6)

½ teaspoon salt

1 tablespoon baking powder

½ teaspoon xanthan gum

¾ cup milk (fat-free can be used)

2 teaspoons pure vanilla extract

2 cups of your favorite frosting

1. Preheat oven to 375°F. Position rack in center of oven. Line bottoms of two 8- or 9-inch round cake pans with wax paper or parchment. Very lightly grease and flour sides of pans with baking spray and approximately ½ teaspoon rice flour.

2. Beat butter and sugar in large bowl of electric mixer until light and fluffy. Add eggs one at a time, blending each one in before adding the next. Scrape bowl and beaters. Add flour, salt, baking powder, xanthan gum, milk, and vanilla; beat at medium speed for 1 minute.

3. Pour batter into prepared pans. Place in center of oven and bake for about 25 minutes for 8-inch rounds (20 minutes for 9-inch rounds) or until a toothpick inserted into center comes out clean.

4. Cool on rack for 7 minutes. Use a small knife to cut around pan sides to loosen cake. Invert cake layers onto a rack, peel off paper, and cool completely.

5. Place one cake layer on a platter. Spread 1 cup of frosting over top and sides. Place second layer on top. Spread remaining frosting over entire cake.

Serve slightly chilled or at room temperature. Can be made a day ahead. Store frosted cake in refrigerator. Unfrosted cake layers can be covered tightly with plastic wrap and stored in refrigerator for one day. Unfrosted cake layers can also be covered with plastic wrap and then with foil and stored in freezer for up to three weeks. Best when eaten within three days of baking.

To make a four-layer cake, chill unfrosted layers until very cold or freeze briefly. Slice horizontally across each layer.

LEMON LAYER CAKE

Makes two 8- or 9-inch rounds or 24 cupcakes. Recipe can be cut in half

Lemon layer cake was one of my Father's favorite birthday cakes when I was little, and I have always loved it as well. This cake is bursting with lemon flavor featured in a variety of melt-in-your-mouth textures: velvety cake, creamy buttercream, and a cool pudding-like lemon curd filling. But don't wait for a birthday party. Make this delicious cake for the lemon lover in your life. It can help turn any meal into a celebration.

Serve slightly chilled or at room temperature. Can be made a day ahead. Store frosted cake in refrigerator. Unfrosted cake layers can be covered tightly with plastic wrap and stored in refrigerator for one day. Unfrosted cake layers can also be covered with plastic wrap and then with foil and stored in freezer for up to three weeks. Best when eaten within three days of baking.

2 cups granulated sugar

4 large eggs

2½ cups Brown Rice Flour Mix (see p. 6)

½ teaspoon salt

1 tablespoon baking powder

1 teaspoon xanthan gum

1 cup canola oil

1 cup milk

1 teaspoon pure vanilla extract

1 teaspoon pure lemon extract

1 tablespoon grated lemon rind

Lemon Curd Filling and Lemon Buttercream Frosting (recipes follow)

1. Preheat oven to 350°F. Position rack in center of oven. Line two round 9-inch layer cake pans with parchment or waxed paper and spray lightly with cooking spray.

2. Beat sugar and eggs in large bowl of electric mixer at medium speed for 1 minute. Add flour, salt, baking powder, xanthan gum, oil, milk, vanilla extract, lemon extract, and lemon rind; beat at medium speed for 1 minute.

3. Pour batter into prepared pans. Place in center of oven and bake about 35 minutes (40 minutes for an 8-inch cake; 18–20 minutes for cupcakes) or until center springs back when touched and cake has pulled away from sides of pan.

4. Cool cake layers in the pans on a rack for 5 minutes. Use a small knife to cut around pan sides to loosen cake. Invert cake layers onto a rack, peel off paper, and cool completely.

5. Carefully slice each layer in half horizontally to create four layers (this is more easily done when cake has been chilled). Spread each

of the two bottom layers with $\frac{1}{2}$ of the lemon curd. Cover each bottom layer with one of the two remaining top layers.

6. Place one set of filled layers on a cake plate and spread with about $\frac{1}{2}$ cup frosting. Place the other set of filled layers on top and cover top and sides of cake with remaining frosting.

LEMON CURD FILLING

3 egg yolks
$\frac{1}{4}$ cup plus 2 tablespoons granulated sugar
$\frac{1}{4}$ cup fresh lemon juice
$\frac{1}{4}$ cup unsalted butter, cut into 4 pieces
$\frac{1}{4}$ teaspoon guar gum*
2 teaspoons grated lemon rind
$\frac{1}{4}$ teaspoon lemon extract

1. Combine egg yolks, sugar, and lemon juice in a small saucepan and whisk until well blended.

2. Cook over medium-low heat until smooth and so thick that curd coats the back of a wooden spoon (this should take 5–7 minutes). Whisk in butter, one piece at a time, until completely incorporated. Whisk in guar gum, lemon rind, and lemon extract.

3. Pour the curd into a small bowl and cover with wax paper or plastic wrap. Chill until very cold.

LEMON BUTTERCREAM FROSTING

1 cup unsalted butter
$3\frac{1}{2}$ cups confectioner's sugar, divided
$\frac{1}{4}$ cup fresh lemon juice
$\frac{1}{2}$ teaspoon lemon extract
2 teaspoons grated lemon rind

1. Beat butter in large bowl of electric mixer until light and fluffy. Add 1 cup confectioner's sugar, lemon juice, lemon extract, and lemon rind; beat to blend. Add remaining sugar and beat until creamy.

Guar gum will add viscosity to the curd and thereby keep it from seeping into the cake layers. You would not use guar gum in a lemon curd tart. It is not necessary to use it here, but the end result will be better.

MAPLE WALNUT CAKE

Makes two 8- or
9-inch rounds.
Recipe can be
cut in half

Maple Walnut Cake is a much-requested favorite in my house. This cake blends the taste of sweet summer apricots with autumn walnuts and winter-rich maple flavor. I tend to make it in the cooler months because the flavors are so warm; it is comfort food in the truest sense.

    2 cups granulated sugar

    4 large eggs

    2½ cups Brown Rice Flour Mix (see p. 6)

    ½ teaspoon salt

    1 tablespoon baking powder

    1 teaspoon xanthan gum

    1 cup canola oil

    1 cup milk

    2 teaspoons pure vanilla extract

    ⅔–1 cup apricot butter *or* preserves*

        Maple Buttercream Frosting (recipe follows)

    2 cups crushed walnuts

Serve slightly chilled or
at room temperature.
Can be made a day
ahead. Store frosted
cake in refrigerator.
Unfrosted cake layers
can be covered tightly
with plastic wrap and
stored in refrigerator
for one day. Unfrosted
cake layers can be cov-
ered with plastic wrap
and then with foil and
stored in freezer for up
to three weeks. Best
when eaten within
three days of baking.

* We recommend
Simon Fischer®
Golden Apricot Butter

1. Preheat oven to 350°F. Position rack in center of oven. Line two 9-inch round layer cake pans with parchment or waxed paper and spray lightly with cooking spray.

2. Beat sugar and eggs in large bowl of electric mixer at medium speed for 1 minute. Add flour, salt, baking powder, xanthan gum, oil, milk, and vanilla; beat at medium speed for 1 minute.

3. Pour batter into prepared pans. Place in center of oven and bake for 35 minutes (40 minutes for an 8-inch cake) or until center springs back when touched and cake has pulled away from sides of pan.

4. Cool cake layers in the pans on a rack for 5 minutes. Use a small knife to cut around pan sides to loosen cake. Invert cake layers onto a rack, peel off paper, and cool completely.

5. Carefully slice each layer in half to create four layers (this is more easily done when cake has been chilled). Spread each of the two bottom layers with ⅓ to ½ cup apricot butter or preserves. Cover each bottom layer with one of the two remaining top layers.

6. Place one set of filled layers on a cake plate and spread with about ½ cup frosting. Place the other set of filled layers on top and cover top and sides of cake with remaining frosting. Gently press crushed walnuts onto top and sides of cake.

MAPLE BUTTERCREAM FROSTING

   1 cup unsalted butter

   3 cups confectioner's sugar, divided

   2 tablespoons very strong black coffee

   1 tablespoon maple extract

   1 tablespoon milk

1. Beat butter in large bowl of electric mixer until light and fluffy. Add 1 cup confectioner's sugar, coffee, and maple extract; beat to blend. Add remaining sugar and milk and beat until creamy.

COCONUT LAYER CAKE

Makes two 8- or 9-inch
rounds or 24 cupcakes.
Recipe can be
cut in half

Luscious coconut cakes. You see them proudly displayed in quaint cafes,
on the long tables of church suppers, and on the covers of food magazines.
Many of us have a favorite recipe, and this is mine. I created it years ago,
and it converted beautifully to its new gluten-free form. I happily make it
for my coconut-loving friends whenever I can.

> 2 cups granulated sugar
>
> 4 large eggs
>
> 2½ cups Brown Rice Flour Mix (see p. 6)
>
> ½ teaspoon salt
>
> 1 tablepoon baking powder
>
> 1 teaspoon xanthan gum
>
> 1 cup canola oil
>
> 1 cup unsweetened coconut milk (not low fat)
>
> 1 teaspoon pure vanilla extract
>
> 1 teaspoon coconut extract
>
> Coconut Frosting (recipe follows)
>
> ½–¾ cup sweetened flaked coconut (optional)

*Serve slightly chilled or
at room temperature.
Can be made a day
ahead. Store frosted
cake in refrigerator.
Unfrosted cake layers
can be covered tightly
with plastic wrap and
stored in refrigerator
for one day. Unfrosted
cake layers can also be
covered with plastic
wrap and then with
foil and stored in
freezer for up to three
weeks. Best when
eaten within three
days of baking.*

*To make a four-layer
cake, chill unfrosted
layers until very cold
or freeze briefly. Slice
horizontally across
each layer.*

1. Preheat oven to 350°F. Position rack in center of oven. Line two
   8-inch round layer cake pans with parchment or waxed paper and
   spray lightly with cooking spray.

2. Beat sugar and eggs in large bowl of electric mixer at medium speed
   for 1 minute. Add flour, salt, baking powder, xanthan gum, oil,
   coconut milk, and vanilla and coconut extracts; beat at medium
   speed for 1 minute.

3. Pour batter into prepared pans. Place in center of oven and bake
   about 40 minutes (35 minutes for a 9-inch cake; 18–20 minutes for
   cupcakes) or until center springs back when touched and cake has
   pulled away from sides of pan.

4. Cool cake layers in the pans on a rack for 5 minutes. Use a small
   knife to cut around pan sides to loosen cake. Invert cake layers onto
   a rack, peel off paper, and cool completely.

5. Place one cake layer on a platter. Spread 1 cup of frosting over top
   and sides. Place second layer on top. Spread remaining frosting over
   entire cake. Pat sweetened flaked coconut onto the sides of the cake.

COCONUT FROSTING

$\frac{1}{2}$ cup unsalted butter, room temperature

4 ozs. low-fat cream cheese, room temperature

3 cups confectioner's sugar, sifted if lumpy

$\frac{1}{4}$ cup unsweetened coconut milk

$\frac{1}{2}$ teaspoon pure vanilla extract

$\frac{1}{2}$ teaspoon coconut extract

1. Beat butter and cream cheese in large bowl of electric mixer until light and fluffy.
2. Add confectioner's sugar, coconut milk, vanilla, and coconut extract and beat at low speed until well blended and smooth.

CHOCOLATE FUDGE CAKE

Makes two 8- or 9-inch rounds or 24 cupcakes. Recipe can be cut in half

If your mouth has been watering for an old-fashioned chocolate layer cake, then here is just the thing: moist and dense but not heavy; rich and fudgy but not too sweet. If you follow these easy directions, you can whip up this cake in no time. Even better, no one will be able to tell it is gluten-free. You can make it for a special celebration, use the batter to make cupcakes for birthday parties (bake about 20 minutes), or make it just because you've been craving a fabulous piece of cake. Pour yourself a cold glass of milk or a hot, steamy cup of coffee and dig in!

4 ozs. unsweetened chocolate, chopped

1¾ cups Brown Rice Flour Mix (see p. 6)

¼ cup unsweetened cocoa powder

2 teaspoons baking powder

1 teaspoon baking soda

½ teaspoon salt

¾ teaspoon xanthan gum

½ cup canola oil

1½ cups fat-free milk

2 cups granulated sugar

2 large eggs

2 teaspoons pure vanilla extract

2 cups of your favorite frosting

Serve slightly chilled or at room temperature. Can be made a day ahead. Store frosted cake in refrigerator. Unfrosted cake layers can be covered tightly with plastic wrap and stored in refrigerator for one day. Unfrosted cake layers can also be covered with plastic wrap and then with foil and stored in freezer for up to two weeks. Best when eaten within three days of baking.

To make a four-layer cake, chill unfrosted layers until very cold or freeze briefly. Slice horizontally across each layer.

1. Preheat oven to 350°F. Position rack in center of oven. Line two 9-inch round layer cake pans with parchment or waxed paper and spray lightly with cooking spray.

2. Melt chocolate in small, heavy saucepan over low heat, stirring constantly. Remove from heat and cool until lukewarm.

3. Put flour, cocoa powder, baking powder, baking soda, salt, and xanthan gum in medium bowl and whisk until thoroughly combined. Set aside.

4. Place canola oil and milk in a liquid measuring cup and whisk until thoroughly combined. Remove two tablespoons of liquid and discard. Set aside.

5. Beat sugar and eggs in large bowl of electric mixer at medium speed until light and fluffy. Blend in melted chocolate and vanilla. Add dry and wet ingredients in two additions at low speed, then mix at medium speed for 1 more minute.

6. Pour batter into prepared pans. Place in center of oven and bake for 30–35 minutes or until a toothpick inserted in the center of a layer comes out clean. (Bake 35–40 minutes for 8-inch rounds; 18–20 minutes for cupcakes).

7. Cool cake layers in the pans on a rack for 5 minutes. Use a small knife to cut around pan sides to loosen cake. Invert cake layers onto a rack, peel off paper, and cool completely.

8. Place one cake layer on a platter. Spread 1 cup of frosting over top and sides. Place second layer on top. Spread remaining frosting over entire cake.

GERMAN CHOCOLATE CAKE

Makes two
9-inch rounds.
Recipe can be
cut in half

Chocolate and coconut together? It doesn't get better than this cake. In fact, it is so good in its new gluten-free form that no one will even notice the lack of wheat, much less miss it. Serve this fabulous German Chocolate Cake after tangy summer barbecues or savory cold-weather stews. No matter when you bring it to the table, it will evoke big smiles.

> 6 ozs. baker's German sweet chocolate, chopped
> $\frac{1}{2}$ cup water
> $2\frac{1}{4}$ cups Brown Rice Flour Mix (see p. 6)
> 2 teaspoons baking soda
> $\frac{1}{4}$ teaspoon salt
> 1 teaspoon xanthan gum
> $\frac{1}{4}$ cup buttermilk powder
> 1 cup canola oil
> $\frac{3}{4}$ cup plus 2 tablespoons water
> 4 large eggs
> 2 cups granulated sugar
> 2 teaspoons pure vanilla extract
> $1\frac{1}{3}$ cups semisweet chocolate chips, divided
> German Chocolate Cake Frosting (recipe follows)

Serve slightly chilled or at room temperature. Can be made a day ahead. Store frosted cake in refrigerator. Unfrosted cake layers can be covered tightly with plastic wrap and stored in refrigerator for one day. Frosted and unfrosted cake layers can be covered with plastic wrap and then with foil and stored in freezer for up to three weeks. Best when eaten within three days of baking.

1. Preheat oven to 350°F. Position rack in center of oven. Line two 9-inch round layer cake pans with parchment or waxed paper and spray with cooking spray.

2. Bring $\frac{1}{2}$ cup water to a simmer in a small saucepan. Turn off heat. Add chopped chocolate and whisk until smooth. Remove from heat and cool until lukewarm.

3. Put flour, baking soda, salt, xanthan gum, and buttermilk powder in medium bowl and whisk until thoroughly combined. Set aside. Combine oil and water in a glass measuring cup. Set aside.

4. Beat eggs in large bowl of electric mixer until lemon colored. Slowly add sugar a little at a time, and beat until mixture turns pale yellow and thick. Beat in melted chocolate and vanilla.

5. Add flour mixture alternately with oil and water mixture in two additions; scrape sides and bottom of bowl, then mix at medium speed for 1 more minute.

6. Pour batter into prepared pans. Sprinkle chocolate chips over the batter in each pan, $\frac{1}{2}$ cup in each (1 cup total). Place pans in center of oven and bake 40–45 minutes or until a toothpick inserted in the center of a layer comes out clean.

7. Cool cake layers in the pans on a rack for 8 minutes. Use a small knife to cut around pan sides to loosen cake. Invert cake layers onto a rack, peel off paper, and cool completely.

8. Frost cake layers separately. Place one cake layer on a platter. Spread $\frac{1}{2}$ of the frosting over top (and sides, if desired). Place second layer on another platter and repeat. Place second layer on top of first. Sprinkle remaining chocolate chips over top of cake.

GERMAN CHOCOLATE CAKE FROSTING

1 12-oz. can evaporated milk
$1\frac{1}{2}$ cups granulated sugar
$\frac{1}{2}$ cup unsalted butter
4 large egg yolks
$\frac{1}{4}$–$\frac{1}{2}$ teaspoon almond extract (to taste)
1 7-oz. package sweetened shredded coconut
$1\frac{1}{2}$ cups coarsely chopped pecans

1. Combine evaporated milk, sugar, butter, and egg yolks in a medium saucepan. Whisk over medium-high heat until mixture is smooth and thick enough to see an indentation from your finger on a frosting-coated wooden spoon. This will take about 15 minutes.

2. Stir in almond extract, coconut, and pecans. Allow to sit at room temperature for one hour before frosting cake.

FLOURLESS CHOCOLATE CAKE

Makes one 9-inch round cake

There is a wonderful variety of flourless chocolate cakes for us to enjoy. Some are heavy and dense and use incredible quantities of melted chocolate. Some feature ground nuts or fruit flavors. Mine has a light soufflé-like texture and a rich chocolate flavor that is almost brownie-like. Serve it with sweetened whipped cream and fresh berries on the side. This cake is utterly simple to make, delightful to eat, and sure to become a favorite.

> 8 ozs. semisweet chocolate
>
> 8 tablespoons unsalted butter, room temperature
>
> ¾ cup granulated sugar
>
> 7 large eggs, separated, room temperature
>
> 1 teaspoon pure vanilla extract

Serve at room temperature. Cake can be made ahead up to two days before serving. Wrap tightly in plastic to refrigerate. Bring to room temperature before serving.

1. Preheat oven to 350°F. Position rack in center of oven. Line 9-inch springform pan with parchment or wax paper and spray lightly with cooking spray.

2. Melt chocolate in small, heavy saucepan over low heat, stirring constantly. Remove from heat and cool until lukewarm.

3. Beat butter and sugar in electric mixer 4–5 minutes. Add egg yolks, one at a time, beating after each addition. Beat in the chocolate and vanilla.

4. Using clean beaters and another large bowl, beat egg whites until soft peaks form. Use a spatula to fold ⅓ of the egg whites into the batter to lighten it. Then fold in remaining egg whites.

5. Pour batter into prepared pan and bake in center of oven for 40–45 minutes or until cake is puffed and the center is firm and elastic to touch.

6. Cool cake in pan for 5 minutes (cake will fall). Use a small knife to cut around pan sides to loosen cake. Remove sides of pan and invert the cake onto a rack. Peel off paper. Cool completely and slide onto a plate.

ANGEL FOOD CAKE

If you know and miss the pleasures of angel food cake, try this fabulous gluten-free version. It looks, tastes, and feels as good as most wheat-containing angel food, and better than those chemically preserved cakes you see in your grocery store. Lacking butter, oil, and egg yolks, all angel food cakes rely on sugar to keep them moist. They are slightly less tender than their sponge counterparts because the egg whites give them so much structure. No matter, you will still need guar gum or xanthan gum to ensure a successful gluten-free cake. Guar gum results in a slightly more tender cake, but xanthan gum will still give you a good texture. So crack some eggs today and start baking!

*Makes one
10-inch cake*

1¼ cups confectioner's sugar

1 cup Brown Rice Flour Mix (see p. 6), *sifted 3 times
before measuring*

½ teaspoon guar gum *or* xanthan gum if guar gum
is unavailable

1½ cups egg whites, room temperature (about 12 egg whites)

1½ teaspoons cream of tartar

¼ teaspoon salt

2 teaspoons pure vanilla extract

½ teaspoon pure almond extract

1 cup granulated sugar

*Serve at room temper-
ature. Can be made
a day ahead. Cover
tightly with plastic
wrap to store in
refrigerator. Cannot
be frozen. Best when
eaten within three
days of baking.*

1. Preheat oven to 400°F. Position rack on second shelf from bottom. Have ready a clean 10-inch tube pan with a removable bottom.

2. Combine and then sift confectioner's sugar, flour, and guar gum into a small bowl and set aside.

3. Combine egg whites, cream of tartar, salt, vanilla, and almond extract in large bowl of electric mixer. Start mixer at medium speed and beat until whites are foamy. Gradually increase speed to high. Add sugar 2 tablespoons at a time, beating until sugar dissolves and whites form stiff peaks. Do not scrape bowl while beating.

4. Fold flour mixture into egg whites in three additions, using a rubber spatula. Pour batter into ungreased 10-inch tube pan. Use the spatula to break any air bubbles and smooth the batter.

5. Place cake in oven and turn down oven temperature to 375°. Bake about 35 minutes or until top of cake springs back when lightly touched with finger and any cracks on surface look dry.

6. Invert cake in pan on funnel or narrow-necked bottle (an empty wine bottle is perfect for this); cool completely. Loosen cake with sharp knife and remove from pan onto a serving plate.

VANILLA SPONGE CAKE OR JELLY ROLL

Makes two 8- or 9-inch rounds or one 15-inch jelly roll. Recipe can be cut in half

Light, delectable sponge cake is a classic dessert that you can use in many delicious ways. Make strawberry shortcake, jelly rolls, and cakes filled with lemon curd, flavored custards, or whipped cream. Follow the directions carefully and you will get a flavorful sponge with a fabulous texture.

$\frac{3}{4}$ cup Brown Rice Flour Mix (see p. 6)

$\frac{1}{2}$ teaspoon baking powder

$\frac{1}{4}$ teaspoon guar gum *or* xanthan gum if guar gum is unavailable

$\frac{1}{8}$ teaspoon salt

6 large eggs, separated, at room temperature

$\frac{3}{4}$ cup granulated sugar, divided

2 teaspoons pure vanilla extract

$\frac{1}{4}$ teaspoon pure almond extract

1. Preheat oven to 350°F. Position rack in center of oven. Line two 8-inch round layer cake pans with parchment or waxed paper and spray very lightly with cooking spray. If making a jelly roll cake, line a 10 $\frac{1}{2}$ x 15 $\frac{1}{2}$-inch jelly roll pan with parchment or waxed paper and spray very lightly with cooking spray.

2. Whisk flour, baking powder, guar gum, and salt together in a small bowl. Set aside.

3. Beat egg whites in large bowl of electric mixer. Start mixer at medium speed and beat until whites are foamy. Gradually increase speed to high. Add $\frac{1}{4}$ cup of the sugar, 1 tablespoon at a time, beating until sugar dissolves and whites form medium soft peaks. Do not scrape bowl while beating. Set aside.

4. Beat egg yolks in large bowl of electric mix until thick and lemon colored. Add remaining $\frac{1}{2}$ cup sugar gradually, 1 tablespoon at a time, and continue to beat until light colored and fluffy. Add flour mixture, vanilla extract, and almond extract and mix until smooth. Batter will be thick.

5. Fold $\frac{1}{3}$ of the beaten egg whites into the batter to lighten it; gently fold in remaining egg whites. Pour batter into cake pans and place in center of preheated oven. Bake 20–22 minutes (8-inch round) or

until cake springs back when touched lightly (bake 18–20 minutes for 9-inch rounds, and 16–18 minutes for 10 $\frac{1}{2}$ x 15 $\frac{1}{2}$-inch jelly roll).

6. *For cake rounds:* Use a small knife to cut around pan sides to loosen cake. Invert pans onto a rack. Peel off paper. Cool completely before filling or frosting.

For jelly roll: Invert pan onto a clean dish towel. Peel off paper. Roll cake and towel together into a roll and place on rack to cool. Cool completely before filling or frosting.

Serve at room temperature or slightly chilled. Can be made a day ahead. Store frosted cake in refrigerator. Unfrosted cake layers can be covered tightly with plastic wrap and stored in refrigerator for one day. Unfrosted cake layers can also be covered with plastic wrap and then with foil and stored in freezer for up to three weeks. Best when eaten within three days of baking.

CHOCOLATE SPONGE CAKE OR JELLY ROLL

Makes two 8- or 9-inch rounds or one 15-inch jelly roll. Recipe can be cut in half

Chocolate sponge cake is one of those classic desserts that you will want in your baking repertoire. Use this light, flavorful sponge to make Yule Logs for the holidays or cakes filled with whipped cream and berries for special celebrations. It is easy to make; just follow the directions carefully and let your imagination go as you create your own special treats.

$\frac{1}{3}$ cup plus 1 tablespoon Brown Rice Flour Mix (see p. 6)

$\frac{1}{3}$ cup unsweetened cocoa powder

$\frac{1}{2}$ teaspoon baking powder

$\frac{1}{4}$ teaspoon guar gum *or* xanthan gum if guar gum is unavailable

$\frac{1}{8}$ teaspoon salt

6 large eggs, separated, at room temperature

$\frac{3}{4}$ cup granulated sugar, divided

2 teaspoons pure vanilla extract

1. Preheat oven to 350°F. Position rack in center of oven. Line two 8-inch round layer cake pans with parchment or waxed paper and spray very lightly with cooking spray. If making a jelly roll cake, line a 10$\frac{1}{2}$ x 15$\frac{1}{2}$-inch jelly roll pan with parchment or waxed paper and spray very lightly with cooking spray.

2. Whisk flour, cocoa powder, baking powder, guar gum, and salt together in a small bowl. Set aside.

3. Beat egg whites in large bowl of electric mixer. Start mixer at medium speed and beat until whites are foamy. Gradually increase speed to high. Add $\frac{1}{4}$ cup of the sugar, 1 tablespoon at a time, beating until sugar dissolves and whites form medium soft peaks. Do not scrape bowl while beating. Set aside.

4. Beat egg yolks in large bowl of electric mixer until thick and lemon colored. Add remaining $\frac{1}{2}$ cup sugar gradually, 1 tablespoon at a time, and continue to beat until light colored and fluffy. Add flour mixture and vanilla extract and mix until smooth. Batter will be thick.

5. Fold $\frac{1}{3}$ of the beaten egg whites into the batter to lighten it; gently fold in remaining egg whites. Pour batter into cake pans and place in center of preheated oven. Bake for 20–22 minutes (8-inch round) or until cake springs back when touched lightly (bake 18–20 minutes for 9-inch rounds, and 16–20 minutes for 10$\frac{1}{2}$ x 15$\frac{1}{2}$-inch jelly roll).

6. *For cake rounds:* Use a small knife to cut around pan sides to loosen cake. Invert the pans onto a rack. Peel off paper. Cool completely before filling or frosting.

For jelly roll: Invert the pans onto a clean dish towel. Peel off paper. Roll cake and towel together into a roll and place on rack to cool for 30 minutes. Unroll and cool completely before filling or frosting.

Serve at room temperature or slightly chilled. Can be made a day ahead. Store frosted cake in refrigerator. Unfrosted cake layers can be covered tightly with plastic wrap and stored in refrigerator for one day. Unfrosted cake layers can also be covered with plastic wrap and then with foil and stored in freezer for up to three weeks. Best when eaten within three days of baking.

CARROT CAKE

*Makes two
9-inch rounds.
Recipe can be
cut in half*

Carrot cake is a traditional favorite that you can find in most cookbooks and magazines. My version is made with fresh shredded carrots, sweetened coconut, crunchy walnuts, and a bit of cinnamon and nutmeg. I recreated it in a fabulous new gluten-free form that is so good my family and friends couldn't tell the difference. Give it a try; it could become a new favorite of yours.

3 cups Brown Rice Flour Mix (see p. 6)

1½ teaspoons xanthan gum

1 tablepoon baking powder

2 teaspoons baking soda

1 teaspoon salt

2 teaspoons cinnamon

½ teaspoon nutmeg

2 cups granulated sugar

1½ cups canola oil

4 large eggs

2 teaspoons pure vanilla extract

2 cups grated, peeled carrots

1 cup chopped walnuts

1 cup shredded sweetened coconut

Cream Cheese Icing (recipe follows)

½ cup toasted sweetened flaked coconut for garnish*

** Spread sweetened
flaked coconut in a
thin layer on a small
baking tray. Bake in
preheated 350°F oven,
stirring every few
minutes until light
golden brown. This
will only take a few
minutes. Don't leave
the oven!*

1. Preheat oven to 350°F. Position rack in center of oven. Line two 9-inch round layer cake pans with parchment or waxed paper and spray lightly with cooking spray.

2. Place flour, xanthan gum, baking soda, baking powder, salt, cinnamon, and nutmeg in medium mixing bowl and whisk until thoroughly combined. Set aside.

3. Beat sugar, oil, and eggs in large bowl of electric mixer until smooth, about 1 minute. Add vanilla and mix well.

4. Pour flour mixture into the sugar and oil mixture and beat at medium-low speed for 1 minute. Fold in carrots, walnuts, and coconut.

5. Pour batter into prepared pans and bake in center of oven for 40 minutes or until a toothpick inserted in center of cake comes out clean.

6. Cool cake layers in the pans on a rack for 10 minutes. Use a small knife to cut around pan sides to loosen cake. Invert cake layers onto a rack, peel off paper, and cool completely.

7. Place one cake layer on platter. Spread 1 cup frosting over top and sides. Place second layer on top. Spread remaining frosting over entire cake. Sprinkle toasted coconut over the top or press onto sides.

CREAM CHEESE ICING

$\frac{1}{2}$ cup unsalted butter, room temperature

$\frac{1}{2}$ cup low-fat cream cheese, room temperature

3 cups confectioner's sugar, sifted if lumpy

1 teaspoon pure vanilla extract

1 lemon, grated and juiced

1. Beat butter and cream cheese in large bowl of electric mixer until light and fluffy.

2. Add confectioner's sugar and beat at low speed until well blended. Beat in vanilla, grated lemon rind, and lemon juice until smooth.

Serve slightly chilled or at room temperature. Can be made a day ahead. Store frosted cake in refrigerator. Unfrosted cake layers can be covered tightly with plastic wrap and stored in refrigerator for one day. Unfrosted cake layers can be covered with plastic wrap and then with foil and stored in freezer for up to three weeks. Best when eaten within three days of baking.

GINGERBREAD

Makes one 8 x 8-inch
square cake or 9-inch
kugelhoph crown-
shaped mold (fluted
ring mold)*

*Can be made a day
ahead. Store
Gingerbread in refrig-
erator, covered tightly
with plastic wrap.
Gingerbread can be
covered with plastic
wrap and then with
foil and stored in
freezer for up to three
weeks. Best when
eaten within three
days of baking.*

** Use a 9-inch kugel-
hoph crown-shaped
mold or a fluted ring
mold that would hold
8 to 10 cups filled to
the top rim. Do not
use a flat-bottomed
tube pan.*

On a cold winter day there is nothing more comforting than the sweet smell of gingerbread baking in the oven. My original recipe, converted to gluten-free, makes a traditional-style cake that features a delicate blend of ginger, cinnamon, and molasses. Dust it with a little powdered sugar and you've got a quick dessert. I like to serve this gingerbread with homemade applesauce on the side.

$1\frac{2}{3}$ cups Brown Rice Flour Mix (see p. 6)

$1\frac{1}{4}$ teaspoons baking soda

$\frac{3}{4}$ teaspoon xanthan gum

$1\frac{1}{2}$ teaspoons ground ginger

$\frac{3}{4}$ teaspoon cinnamon

$\frac{3}{4}$ teaspoon salt

1 large egg, lightly beaten

$\frac{1}{2}$ cup granulated sugar

$\frac{1}{2}$ cup molasses

$\frac{1}{2}$ cup canola oil

$\frac{1}{2}$ cup boiling water

Confectioner's sugar

1. Preheat oven to 350°F. Position rack in center of oven. Lightly spray a kugelhoph mold with cooking spray.

2. Place flour, baking soda, xanthan gum, ginger, cinnamon, and salt in large bowl of electric mixer and mix at low speed until thoroughly combined.

3. Add egg, sugar, and molasses and mix until smooth, about 1 minute. Pour oil and boiling water over batter and mix until smooth, about 30 seconds.

4. Pour batter into prepared pan and bake in center of oven for 40 minutes or until top springs back when touched and a toothpick inserted in center of cake comes out clean (bake 35 minutes for 8 x 8-inch square).

5. Cool cake in pan on a rack for 5 minutes. Use a small knife to cut around pan sides to loosen cake if necessary. Invert cake onto a rack and cool. Sift confectioner's sugar over cake and serve warm (or at room temperature) with applesauce.

NEW YORK CHEESECAKE

There are countless recipes for cheesecakes of all kinds. But to New Yorkers, where cheesecake originated, there is only one kind, and it doesn't have chocolate or pecans or raspberry puree. And it certainly isn't made with fat-free cream cheese and evaporated milk. No, if you are going to have cheesecake, you should have the real thing. And here it is. Just be sure to share it with a lot of friends and family. Take note: This cake should be prepared one day before serving.

Crust

1¼ cups Brown Rice Flour Mix (see p. 6)

1 teaspoon xanthan gum

10 tablespoons unsalted butter, room temperature.

¼ cup granulated sugar

1 large egg yolk

Grated rind of 1 lemon

1. Preheat oven to 350°F. Position rack in center of oven. Spray bottom of 10-inch springform pan with cooking spray. Dust lightly with rice flour.

2. Mix all ingredients for crust in bowl of electric mixer and mix at low speed. Press about ⅓ of dough into detached bottom of springform pan and bake 12 minutes. Cool slightly on rack. While bottom is baking, roll the rest of dough out between two pieces of wax paper and refrigerate. Turn oven control to 475°F.

Cream Cheese Filling

5 8-oz. packages cream cheese*

1¾ cups granulated sugar

3 tablespoons Brown Rice Flour Mix (see p. 6)

¼ teaspoon salt

5 large eggs

2 large egg yolks

2 tablespoons Half and Half *or* whole milk *or* light cream

1 tablespoon grated orange rind

Grated rind of 1 lemon

Makes one 10-inch round cake

Remove from refrigerator one hour before serving. Store in refrigerator for up to five days. Whole cake or sections can be tightly covered with plastic wrap and then with foil and stored in freezer for up to one month.

* Philadelphia® Original Cream Cheese is best.

1. To make filling, beat cream cheese until smooth in large bowl of electric mixer at medium speed. Reduce speed and slowly add sugar, then flour, salt, eggs, egg yolks, Half and Half, and orange and lemon rind. Scrape bowl and beaters; beat at high speed for 5 more minutes.

2. Attach bottom of springform pan to sides. Press remaining dough around sides to within 1 inch of top of pan. Pour cream cheese filling into pan. Bake in center of oven for 12 minutes; turn oven control down to 300°F and bake 50 minutes more. Turn off oven, but do not open door; leave cake in oven another 15 minutes. Cool cake on wire rack and refrigerate. When cold, remove pan sides and slide cheesecake off bottom onto a platter. Serve with sliced fresh strawberries.

CLASSIC CHEESECAKE

This classic cheesecake is slightly less dense than New York style cheesecake but just as creamy and flavorful. Make it with the crust or without; it will be delicious either way. I like to serve slices topped with seasonal fresh fruit or fruit compote. It's easy and fast to make and sure to become a much requested favorite. Take note: Make cheesecake one day before serving.

Makes one 9-inch round cake

Crust

> 1 cup Brown Rice Flour Mix (see p. 6)
>
> 1 teaspoon xanthan gum
>
> 5 tablespoons unsalted butter
>
> 1/4 cup granulated sugar

1. Preheat oven to 350°F. Position rack in center of oven. Spray bottom of 9-inch round springform pan with cooking spray. Dust lightly with rice flour.

2. Place flour, xanthan gum, butter, and sugar in bowl of electric mixer. Mix on low speed until crumbly. Press into detached bottom of springform pan.

3. Bake in center of oven for 12 minutes. Remove from oven and set aside. Turn oven control up to 475°F.

Cream Cheese Filling

> 4 8-oz. packages cream cheese*
>
> 1 1/3 cups granulated sugar
>
> 1 tablespoon pure vanilla extract
>
> 4 large eggs
>
> 8 ozs. sour cream (low-fat can be used)
>
> Juice and grated rind of 1 large lemon

1. Beat cream cheese until smooth in bowl of electric mixer at medium speed. Reduce speed and slowly add sugar and vanilla. Beat in eggs one at a time. Scrape bowl and beaters. Add sour cream, lemon juice, and grated lemon rind and mix until well blended.

2. Attach bottom of springform pan to sides. Pour cream cheese batter into pan. Bake in center of oven for 10 minutes; turn oven control down to 200°F and bake 1 hour more. Turn off oven, but do not open door; leave cake in oven for another 15 minutes. Cool cake on wire rack and refrigerate. When cold, remove sides and slide cheesecake off bottom onto a platter. Serve with fresh fruit.

Remove from refrigerator one hour before serving. Store in refrigerator for up to five days. Whole cake or sections can be tightly covered with plastic wrap and then with foil and stored in freezer for up to one month.

* Philadelphia® Original Cream Cheese is best.

CUSTARD CAKE WITH FRUIT

Makes one 9-inch cake

Custard cakes are common to a great many cuisines, but they go by a variety of names: Clafouti, Far Breton, Pasteis de Nata, Bougatsa—you might even have your own favorite. These cakes are homey comfort food made simple. Fresh fruit and a quickly made batter are baked until a golden, crusty, custardy cake emerges hot from the oven. Serve it warm sprinkled with powdered sugar and you'll have a delicious dessert you can serve after dinner or at a special brunch.

1 large Granny Smith apple *or* 1 large Bosc pear

1 teaspoon unsalted butter

1 teaspoon brown sugar

2 tablespoons calvados *or* cognac

$\frac{1}{2}$ cup Brown Rice Flour Mix (see p. 6)

$\frac{1}{2}$ cup sugar

$\frac{1}{8}$ teaspoon salt

4 large eggs

2 cups whole milk

$1\frac{1}{2}$ teaspoons pure vanilla extract

Confectioner's sugar for garnish

1. Peel and core apple; cut into eight slices. Cut each slice into four chunks. Melt 1 teaspoon butter in a small sauté pan over medium-high heat. Stir in 1 teaspoon brown sugar. Mix in apples and coat with butter mixture. Sauté until light golden brown, stirring constantly. Remove from heat. Pour calvados over apples and ignite; allow flames to burn off. Set aside to cool.

2. Preheat oven to 375°F. Position rack in center of oven. Lightly spray a 9-inch round glass (Pyrex) or ceramic deep-dish pie pan with cooking spray and dust lightly with white rice flour.

3. Whisk flour, sugar, and salt in a large bowl.

4. Break eggs into center of flour mixture and whisk until just smooth. Add milk and vanilla extract and whisk until just smooth.

5. Pour batter into prepared pan. Drop sautéed apples into the batter. Put pan in center of oven; bake about 55 minutes (a knife inserted into center of cake should come out clean). Do not open oven for 45 minutes.

6. Cool cake in the pan on a rack for 1 hour. Sift confectioner's sugar over top.

CUSTARD CAKE WITH CHERRIES

Replacement Step 1. Melt 1 teaspoon butter in a small sauté pan over medium-high heat. Stir in 1 teaspoon brown sugar. Mix in 1 ½ cups pitted cherries and coat with butter mixture. Turn off heat. Pour cognac over cherries and ignite; allow flames to burn off. Proceed with Step 2 above.

Serve warm, at room temperature, or slightly chilled. Can be made a day ahead. Store cake covered tightly with plastic wrap in refrigerator. Best when eaten within three days of baking.

SOUR CREAM COFFEE CAKE

Makes one 9-inch tube cake

Sour cream coffee cake is a traditional offering at holiday brunches and morning coffees. My friend Daria made this one for me years ago and I've never found another that I like better. It converted well to its new gluten-free form: it's still easy to make and yummy. Take note: It may appear that there is not enough batter for two layers. Just be sure to make two very thin layers of batter with the apples and nut mixture in between.

$\frac{1}{2}$ cup chopped walnuts

2 teaspoons cinnamon

$1\frac{1}{2}$ cups sugar, divided

1 medium apple

2 cups Brown Rice Flour Mix (see p. 6)

$1\frac{1}{2}$ teaspoons baking powder

1 teaspoon baking soda

$\frac{3}{4}$ teaspoon xanthan gum

$\frac{1}{2}$ teaspoon salt

2 large eggs, room temperature

2 teaspoons pure vanilla extract

1 cup sour cream, room temperature

$\frac{1}{3}$ cup canola oil

1. Preheat oven to 350°F. Position rack in center of oven. Spray a 9-inch tube pan with removable bottom with cooking spray.

2. Mix walnuts, cinnamon, and $\frac{1}{2}$ cup of sugar in a small bowl. Set aside.

3. Peel and core apple; cut into 8 slices. Cut each slice horizontally into 8 small pieces, not long thin slices. Set aside.

4. Whisk flour, baking powder, baking soda, xanthan gum, and salt together in a small bowl. Set aside.

5. Beat eggs in large bowl of electric mixer until well blended. Add remaining sugar, 1 tablespoon at a time, and beat until creamy-colored and light. Add vanilla, flour mixture, sour cream, and oil and beat at medium-low speed for 30 seconds.

6. Evenly spread $\frac{1}{2}$ of batter into prepared pan. Top with apple pieces and $\frac{1}{2}$ of nut mixture. Evenly spread remaining batter over the top; sprinkle with remaining nut mixture. There is not much batter, so do not be afraid to spread what will appear to be two very thin layers

of batter, with the apples and nut mixture in between; spread with a cake spatula or butter knife. The batter will rise and give you a cake several inches high.

7. Place in center of oven and bake about 50 minutes or until a toothpick inserted in center of cake comes out clean. Do not open oven for 45 minutes.

8. Cool cake in pan on a rack for 20 minutes. Remove sides of pan and cool completely on rack. To remove cake from bottom, use two pancake turners to lift cake onto a cake plate.

Serve slightly chilled or at room temperature. Can be made a day ahead. Store cake covered tightly with plastic wrap in refrigerator. Best when eaten within three days of baking.

VANILLA POUND CAKE

Makes one 9-inch
bundt-shaped cake* or
three 5 x 3-inch loaves

*Serve slightly chilled or
at room temperature.
Can be made a day
ahead. Store cake
covered tightly with
plastic wrap in refrig-
erator. Pound Cake
can be covered with
plastic wrap and then
with foil and stored in
freezer for up to three
weeks. Best when
eaten within four days
of baking.*

** Use a 9-inch (across
top) kugelhoph crown-
shaped mold or a
fluted ring mold that
holds 8 to 10 cups
filled to the top rim.
If you use a 9 x 5-inch
loaf pan, cake will be
dense and heavy. Do
not use a 9-inch flat-
bottomed tube pan or
you will have a 1-inch-
high cake. You can use
mini bundt pans, but
you will need to adjust
baking time.*

Vanilla pound cake is a classic dessert traditionally made with equal parts of butter, sugar, and eggs. But when I started to test gluten-free versions, I quickly realized that using butter would not give me the result I wanted. My gluten-free pound cake uses canola oil and whole-milk yogurt with great effect. In fact, during pound-cake-testing week, I was making several pound cakes a day (to the delight of my kids and testers). I started sending large chunks of pound cake to school with my gluten-tolerant son, who passed big pieces around the lunch table to his friends. Late in the week, I received a call from a mother who said her son wanted my Chocolate Chip version (see below) for his birthday dinner.

So here it is. You *can* make a great pound cake without butter.

1½ cups Brown Rice Flour Mix (see p. 6)
2½ teaspoons baking powder
½ teaspoon xanthan gum
¼ teaspoon salt
3 large eggs
1 cup granulated sugar
1 cup plain whole-milk yogurt
⅓ cup canola oil
2 teaspoons pure vanilla extract
Confectioner's sugar for garnish

1. Preheat oven to 350°F. Position rack in center of oven. Spray a 9-inch bundt pan or kugelhoph mold with cooking spray.

2. Whisk flour, baking powder, xanthan gum, and salt in a small bowl. Set aside.

3. Beat eggs in large bowl of electric mixer at medium-high speed; gradually add sugar 1 tablespoon at a time and beat until light colored and thickened.

4. Add flour mixture, yogurt, oil, and vanilla extract and beat at medium-low speed for 30 seconds.

5. Evenly spread batter into prepared pan. Place in center of oven and bake about 50 minutes (a toothpick inserted in center of cake should come out clean). Do not open oven for 45 minutes.

6. Cool cake in the pan on a rack for 10 minutes. Carefully remove cake from pan and cool completely on rack. Sift confectioner's sugar over top.

CHOCOLATE CHIP POUND CAKE

Stir in ⅔ to ¾ cup semisweet chocolate chips before spreading batter in pan.

LEMON POUND CAKE

Makes one 9-inch bundt-shaped cake* or three 5 x 3-inch loaves

This is the perfect little cake to serve with coffee and tea. It has a bright lemon flavor, a tender crumb, and a velvety texture. Dust it with powdered sugar or dribble a tangy lemon glaze over the top (recipe follows). I also like to make it with fresh blueberries when they are in season or poppy seeds (recipes below). No matter which version you make, you'll have a simple, delicious cake that you'll want to make again and again.

1½ cups Brown Rice Flour Mix (see p. 6)
2½ teaspoons baking powder
½ teaspoon xanthan gum
¼ teaspoon salt
3 large eggs
1 cup granulated sugar
1 cup plain whole-milk yogurt
⅓ cup canola oil
1 teaspoon pure vanilla extract
1 teaspoon pure lemon extract
1 tablespoon grated lemon rind
Confectioner's sugar (optional) for garnish

Serve slightly chilled or at room temperature. Can be made a day ahead. Store cake covered tightly with plastic wrap in refrigerator. Pound Cake can be covered with plastic wrap and then with foil and stored in freezer for up to three weeks. Best when eaten within four days of baking.

* Use a 9-inch (across top) kugelhoph crown-shaped mold or a fluted ring mold that holds 8 to 10 cups filled to the top rim. If you use a 9 x 5-inch loaf pan, cake will be dense and heavy. Do not use a 9-inch flat-bottomed tube pan or you will have a 1-inch-high cake. You can use mini bundt pans, but you will need to adjust baking time.

1. Preheat oven to 350°F. Position rack in center of oven. Spray a 9-inch bundt pan or kugelhoph mold with cooking spray.

2. Whisk flour, baking powder, xanthan gum, and salt together in a small bowl. Set aside.

3. Beat eggs in large bowl of electric mixer at medium-high speed; gradually add sugar, 1 tablespoon at a time, and beat until light colored and thickened.

4. Add flour mixture, yogurt, oil, vanilla extract, lemon extract, and lemon rind and beat at medium-low speed for 30 seconds.

5. Evenly spread batter into prepared pan. Place in center of oven and bake about 50 minutes (a toothpick inserted in center of cake should come out clean). Do not open oven for 45 minutes.

6. Cool cake in the pan on a rack for 10 minutes. Carefully remove cake from pan and cool completely on rack. Sift confectioner's sugar over top or brush on lemon glaze (recipe follows).

LEMON BLUEBERRY POUND CAKE

Stir in ²⁄₃ to ¾ cup fresh dry blueberries before spreading batter in pan.

LEMON POPPY SEED POUND CAKE

Stir in ¹⁄₃ cup poppy seeds before spreading batter in pan.

LEMON GLAZE

¼ cup granulated sugar

2 tablespoons fresh lemon juice

1. Put sugar and lemon juice in small saucepan and whisk over medium-high heat until sugar is dissolved.
2. Use pastry brush to brush glaze on cooled pound cake.

Pies and Tarts

I WAS WORRIED ABOUT making pie crust when I first started trying to convert my treasured recipes to gluten-free. But I worried needlessly. Gluten-free flours make fabulous pie crusts and tart shells. In fact, this is a job they were made for. Crusts made with gluten-free flours taste delicious and stay fresh long after those with wheat have withered into soggy messes. Even juicy fruit pies and lemon meringue pie hold up better with a gluten-free crust.

I have included recipes for several classic pies, all favorites of mine. But you can use the crusts with any of your own family favorites. Just be sure to replace any flour in the filling with cornstarch.

The Traditional Pie Crust rolls out easily, and you will be able to place it into the pie pan without a problem; just follow the directions carefully. This crust is also easy to prepare ahead of time because you can wrap the dough in a flattened ball or roll it out and place it in the pan and then freeze it.

In addition, you won't need to make a cookie crumb crust ever again, and you won't want to once you've tasted my Tart Shell Crust and Chocolate Tart Shell Crust. Both of these crusts work well with cream pies and fruit tarts, and both can be used for the bottom of cheesecakes. Be sure to try the Chocolate Tart Shell Crust for ice cream pie.

This chapter uses the following pans:

- 8- or 9-inch pie pan
- 9- or 10-inch tart shell

THE LAST WORD ON PIE CRUSTS

- Set-up before starting the recipe: assemble all the ingredients
- *Use cold butter*
- Measure carefully (see Chapter 3)
- Use the right size pan or adjust baking time to compensate
- Preheat the oven to the proper temperature (make sure the oven is calibrated correctly)
- Do not open the oven door more than necessary
- Use a timer because you can get distracted

TRADITIONAL PIE CRUST

This is really a fabulous pie crust, perhaps even better than those made with wheat. It stands up well to fruit fillings, custards, even lemon meringue. It is probably the only pie crust you will ever eat that is as good the second day as it is the first.

Makes one 8- or 9-inch pie crust or one 10-inch tart crust

It is easy to make in a mixer—no messy hands or time-consuming pastry cutters. You will become a pie-crust-making phenomenon in your own home. When you make the Traditional Pie Crust, be sure to use the sweet rice flour called for in the recipe. It will help give you a great crust. (I recommend Authentic Foods® sweet rice flour.)

Take note: When you prebake this crust, it is at a lower temperature than is commonly used for pie crusts made with wheat (see directions below). This is to make sure the dough cooks before it browns. If you notice the crust rising in the middle while it is baking, open the oven quickly and prick it once with a small sharp knife. I also suggest that you partially bake this pie crust whenever you are making a fruit pie or quiche.

> 1 cup plus 2 tablespoons Brown Rice Flour Mix (see p. 6)
>
> 2 tablespoons sweet rice flour
>
> 1 tablespoon granulated sugar (omit if using for a savory pie filling)
>
> $\frac{1}{2}$ teaspoon xanthan gum
>
> $\frac{1}{4}$ teaspoon salt
>
> 6 tablespoons cold unsalted butter (not margarine) cut into 6 pieces
>
> 1 large egg
>
> 2 teaspoons orange juice *or* lemon juice

1. Spray 9-inch pie pan or tart pan (with removable bottom) with cooking spray. Generously dust with rice flour.

2. Mix flours, sugar, xanthan gum, and salt in large bowl of electric mixer. Add butter and mix until crumbly and resembling coarse meal.

3. Add egg and orange juice. Mix on low speed until dough holds together; it should not be sticky. Form dough into a ball, using your hands, and place on a sheet of wax paper. Top with a second sheet of wax paper and flatten dough to 1 inch thickness. *Dough can be frozen at this point for up to 1 month; wrap in plastic wrap and then use foil as an outer wrap.*

4. Roll out dough between the 2 sheets of wax paper. If dough seems tacky, refrigerate for 15 minutes before proceeding. Remove top

sheet of wax paper and invert dough into pie pan. Remove remaining sheet of wax paper, and crimp edges for single-crust pie. *Dough can also be frozen at this point for up to 1 month; line pie shell with wax paper, wrap in plastic wrap, and use foil as an outer wrap.*

To prebake a bottom pie crust:

Preheat oven to 375°F. Gently prick pastry in 3 or 4 places with a fork. Bake pastry for about 25 minutes or until golden. Remove from oven and cool completely on a wire rack. *Prebaked pie shells can be stored in airtight plastic containers or plastic wrap in refrigerator for 3 days. For longer storage, wrap in plastic wrap and then in foil, and store in freezer for up to 2 weeks.*

To partially bake a bottom pie crust:

Preheat oven to 375°F. Bake pastry for 10 minutes. Remove from oven. Fill and bake as per recipe.

TART SHELL CRUST

Gluten-free flours make great tart shells. They are crunchy and delicious, and they stay that way for days. This crust is actually a little like the best cookie crumb crust you ever had—but better. You can make it in minutes and then let your imagination go: fruit tarts, key lime tart, lemon curd tart, chocolate cream tart, coconut cream tart, banana cream tart—just dream it up and you can make it. You can also use this crust for the bottom of cheesecakes (prebake 12 minutes at 350°F); it doesn't get soggy like graham cracker crumbs—ever.

> 1 cup Brown Rice Flour Mix (see p. 6)
>
> ¼ cup granulated sugar
>
> 1 teaspoon xanthan gum
>
> 5 tablespoons cold butter
>
> 1 teaspoon pure vanilla extract

1. Preheat oven to 350°F. Position rack in center of oven. Spray 9-inch pie pan or tart pan (with removable bottom) with cooking spray. Generously dust with rice flour.

2. Combine flour, sugar, and xanthan gum in large bowl of electric mixer (or food processor). Add butter and mix (or pulse) on low speed until crumbly. Add vanilla and mix well. Press into bottom and up sides of pie or tart pan.

3. Bake in center of oven for about 18 minutes or until light golden. Cool on rack in pan. For a tart, place pan on top of a broad glass and carefully push down sides. For best results, remove pan sides and bottom once tart shell is filled and chilled.

Makes one 9-inch pie crust or one 9-inch tart crust

Cover with plastic wrap and store in refrigerator. Best when eaten within 3 days of baking.

CHOCOLATE TART SHELL CRUST

Makes one 9-inch pie crust or one 9-inch tart crust

This fabulous pie crust has a rich chocolate flavor and crunchy texture. It stays crunchy and firm better than any chocolate cookie crumb pie crust you have ever eaten. I use it to make chocolate cream pie and ice cream pie, but you can come up with your own favorites. In addition, it is a great recipe to use when kids want to bake something themselves because it's so easy. Let them dream up the perfect ice cream pie for a family celebration.

$\frac{3}{4}$ cup plus 1 tablespoon Brown Rice Flour Mix (see p. 6)

$\frac{1}{3}$ cup granulated sugar

$\frac{1}{4}$ cup unsweetened cocoa powder

$\frac{1}{2}$ teaspoon xanthan gum

$\frac{1}{8}$ teaspoon salt

5 tablespoons cold butter

1 teaspoon pure vanilla extract

Cover with plastic wrap and store in refrigerator. Best when eaten within 3 days of baking.

1. Preheat oven to 350°F. Position rack in center of oven. Generously spray a 9-inch pie pan or tart pan (with removable bottom) with cooking spray. Generously dust with rice flour.

2. Combine flour, sugar, cocoa powder, xanthan gum, and salt in large bowl of electric mixer (or food processor). Add butter and mix (or pulse) on low speed until crumbly. Add vanilla and mix well. Press into bottom and up sides of pie or tart pan.

3. Bake in center of oven for about 18 minutes or until cooked through. Cool on rack in pan. For a tart, place pan on top of a broad glass and carefully push down sides. For best results, remove pan sides and bottom once tart shell is filled and chilled.

APPLE PIE WITH CRUMB TOPPING

Serves 10

What could be more classic than apple pie? This is my favorite recipe for it, and the only one I ever make. I must say it is a better pie with its new gluten-free crust and crumb topping: They don't get soft the second and third day like they did when I made them with wheat. I use a variety of Granny Smith and Yellow Delicious apples, but you can use your own favorites.

> 1 9-inch Traditional Pie Crust (see p. 71), unbaked

Crumb Topping

> ³/₄ cup Brown Rice Flour Mix (see p. 6)
>
> ¹/₂ cup granulated sugar
>
> ¹/₄ teaspoon xanthan gum
>
> ¹/₃ cup unsalted butter, cold and diced

Filling

> 6 cups thinly sliced tart apples
>
> ¹/₂ cup granulated sugar
>
> ¹/₄ cup brown sugar
>
> 1 tablespoon cornstarch
>
> 1 teaspoon cinnamon
>
> ¹/₂ teaspoon nutmeg
>
> 1 tablespoon lemon juice
>
> 1 tablespoon butter

To prepare Pie Crust:

1. Preheat oven to 375°F. Position rack in center of oven. Spray 9-inch pie pan with cooking spray, and generously dust with rice flour. Place pie pastry into pie pan and flute edges. Partially bake crust in oven for 10 minutes. Cool on rack while preparing apples and crumb topping. Turn oven temperature up to 400°F.

To make Crumb Topping:

2. Combine flour, sugar, and xanthan gum in a medium mixing bowl and cut in butter. Topping should resemble cornmeal in texture. Set aside.

Store in refrigerator. Serve chilled or allow pie to come to room temperature. Best when eaten within 4 days of baking.

To make Filling:

3. Mix sliced apples with sugars, cornstarch, cinnamon, nutmeg, and lemon juice in a large mixing bowl. Fill prepared pastry crust with apple mixture, mounding it slightly. Dot with cut-up pieces of butter.

4. Spoon Crumb Topping over apples and pat it down into place. Cover entire pie with foil. Place in center of oven and bake for 30 minutes.

5. Remove foil. Turn oven temperature down to 375°F and bake for 30–40 minutes more or until filling is bubbling and top is golden. If edges of crust are browning too quickly, cover them with more foil. Cool on a rack before serving. Can be made a day ahead.

FRUIT PIES

1 9-inch Traditional Pie Crust (see pp. 71, 72). For top crust, use Crumb Topping (see recipe p. 75) or a second 9-inch Traditional Pie Crust chilled and rolled out between 2 sheets of wax paper

6 cups of berries *or* peeled and sliced fruit.

¾–1 cup of sugar, depending on sweetness of fruit (use granulated sugar *or* a combination of granulated and brown sugar)

1–3 tablespoons cornstarch, depending on moisture content of fruit (fresh berries and peaches will need more, for instance)

Cinnamon, nutmeg, *and/or* ginger (to taste)

1 tablespoon lemon juice

1 tablespoon butter

Serves 10

Store in refrigerator. Serve chilled or allow pie to come to room temperature. Best when eaten within 4 days of baking.

To prepare Pie Crust:

1. Preheat oven to 375°F. Position rack in center of oven. Spray 9-inch pie pan with cooking spray, and generously dust with rice flour. Place pie pastry into pie pan and flute edges. Partially bake crust in oven for 10 minutes. Cool on rack while preparing fruit filling and crumb topping (if using). Turn oven temperature up to 400°F.

To make Filling:

2. Mix fruit with sugar, cornstarch, spices, and lemon juice in a large mixing bowl. Fill prepared pastry crust with fruit mixture, mounding it slightly. Dot with cut-up pieces of butter.

3. Spoon Crumb Topping (if using) over fruit and pat it down into place. Or cover with second prepared pie crust and crimp edges.

For pie with Crumb Topping:

Bake as instructed on p. 76, Steps 4 and 5, but once you turn the oven down to 375°F, adjust baking time based on fruit (fresh blueberries, peaches, and plums will take less time to bake than apples, etc.).

For pie topped with Traditional Pie Crust:

Bake at 375°F for 45–50 minutes or until crust is nicely browned and fruit juices in center of pie are bubbling.

PECAN PIE

Serves 10–12

Pecan pie is a holiday classic. My favorite recipe came from family friend Miriam Sursa, and it never fails to please. It is not too sweet and it's chock full of luscious pecans. But why wait for a holiday to make it? Get baking, and treat yourself and your friends to this delicious pie today.

1 9-inch Traditional Pie Crust (see p. 71), unbaked
1 cup granulated sugar
³⁄₄ cup light corn syrup
¹⁄₄ cup maple syrup
¹⁄₂ cup unsalted butter
¹⁄₂ teaspoon salt
3 large eggs
2 teaspoons pure vanilla extract
2 cups pecans (chopped and whole)

Store in refrigerator. Serve chilled or allow pie to come to room temperature. Best when eaten within 4 days of baking.

1. Preheat oven to 350°F. Position rack in center of oven. Spray 9-inch pie pan with cooking spray, and generously dust with rice flour. Place pie pastry into pie pan and flute edges.

2. Combine sugar, corn syrup, maple syrup, butter, and salt in heavy saucepan over medium heat; stir frequently until sugar is dissolved. Remove from heat.

3. Beat the eggs in a small bowl and quickly whisk into saucepan. Add vanilla and pecans; mix well. Pour into prepared 9-inch pie shell.

4. Bake in center of oven for 45–50 minutes until center is set. If edges of crust are browning too quickly, cover them with foil. Cool on a rack before serving. Can be made a day ahead.

KEY LIME PIE

Key Lime Pie is one of those special desserts that makes people smile. I like to serve it in the summer after a spicy barbecue. But in warm weather I don't want to turn the oven on twice to make one dessert, so I bake my Tart Shell Crust and then cook the filling on the stove, the way you would make any lemon curd.

Take note: This pie does not have a deep filling if you follow the directions as given. Key Lime Pie is somewhat rich, so I tend to keep it small. If you double the filling, as I sometimes do, you may have slightly more than you need, but it makes a nice deep pie.

Serves 8–10

1 prebaked Tart Shell Crust (see p. 73), baked in a 9-inch pie pan or 9-inch tart pan

Filling

½ cup Nellie & Joe's Key West Lime Juice (or other brand of key lime juice; regular lime juice is not the same)

3 large egg yolks

1 14-oz. can sweetened condensed milk

Topping

¾ cup heavy cream

2 tablespoons confectioner's sugar

1½ teaspoons pure vanilla extract

Store in refrigerator. Best when eaten within 3 days of baking.

To make Filling:

1. Combine lime juice and egg yolks in small saucepan. Cook over medium-low heat until thickened and liquid thickly coats back of wooden spoon. Stir constantly. Liquid should simmer but not boil. This should take 5–6 minutes.

2. Remove from heat and stir in sweetened condensed milk. Pour filling into small bowl and press plastic wrap directly onto surface to prevent hardening. Refrigerate until cool.

3. Pour cooled filling into prebaked Tart Shell Crust. If using a tart pan, place pan on top of a broad glass and carefully push down sides of shell. For best results, remove pan bottom once tart shell is filled and chilled.

To make Topping:

4. Combine heavy cream, confectioner's sugar, and vanilla in large bowl of electric mixer; beat until stiff peaks form. Use pastry bag to pipe sweetened heavy cream around edges of pie. Refrigerate pie until well chilled. Serve cold.

CHOCOLATE CREAM PIE

Serves 8–10

I have always loved chocolate cream pie. It is the kind of dessert you get to enjoy after special family dinners. I passed my love for it onto my children, and it has become a favorite in our house. Now, when I make it, it doesn't last long and the leftovers disappear from the refrigerator at an alarming rate. The crunchy chocolate tart shell and the rich, creamy chocolate custard are a winning combination.

> 1 prebaked Chocolate Tart Shell Crust (see p. 74), baked in a 9-inch pie pan or 9-inch tart pan; *or* one prebaked Traditional Pie Crust (see pp. 71, 72), baked in a 9-inch pie pan

Filling

- 4 ozs. semisweet chocolate
- 4 large egg yolks
- ⅔ cup granulated sugar
- ¼ cup cornstarch
- ¼ teaspoon salt
- 2 cups whole milk
- 1 tablespoon unsalted butter
- 1 tablespoon pure vanilla extract

* Use a potato peeler to shave sides of a bar of semisweet chocolate.

Topping

- ¾ cup heavy cream
- 2 tablespoons confectioner's sugar
- 1½ teaspoons pure vanilla extract
- 3 tablespoons shaved semisweet chocolate*

To make Filling:

1. Melt chocolate in small, heavy saucepan over low heat, stirring constantly. Remove from heat and cool until lukewarm.

2. Beat egg yolks in large bowl of electric mixer at medium-high speed until foamy. Gradually add sugar a little at a time and continue beating until the mixture is pale yellow and thick. Add the cornstarch and salt and beat until well blended.

3. Bring milk to a boil in a large, heavy saucepan over medium-high heat while you are beating the egg yolks.

4. With the mixer on low, gradually add hot milk to egg mixture in a thin stream. Quickly scrape sides and bottom of bowl and mix at medium speed until well blended.

5. Pour the custard mixture back into the saucepan and cook it over medium-high heat, stirring constantly with a wire whip, until it comes to a boil and thickens. Lower heat and cook for 1 minute more. Remove from heat and beat in melted chocolate, butter, and vanilla.

6. Place custard in medium bowl or plastic container to cool. Cover with plastic wrap to prevent a skin from forming over the surface and chill in the refrigerator. *Can be stored in refrigerator for up to 5 days or in freezer for up to 1 month in a tightly sealed container. Keep plastic wrap on surface.*

7. Pour cooled chocolate custard into cooled prebaked Chocolate Tart Shell Crust or Traditional Pie Crust.

To make Topping:

8. Combine heavy cream, confectioner's sugar, and vanilla in large bowl of electric mixer; beat until stiff peaks form. Use pastry bag to pipe sweetened heavy cream around edges of pie. Sprinkle shaved chocolate over whipped cream. Refrigerate until well chilled. Serve cold.

Store in refrigerator. Best when eaten within 3 days of baking.

COCONUT CREAM PIE

Serves 10

The best Coconut Cream Pies are usually found in little out-of-the-way restaurants and old inns. In reality, I found them hard to come by even in cookbooks, so I created this recipe years ago. It's full of rich coconut flavor but not too sweet. I like to make it in the crunchy Tart Shell Crust, but traditionalists might prefer the Traditional Pie Crust. No matter which you choose, you'll have a great pie and a lot of requests for second helpings.

> 1 prebaked Tart Shell Crust (see p. 73), baked in a 9-inch pie pan or 9-inch tart pan; *or* 1 prebaked Traditional Pie Crust (see pp. 71, 72), baked in a 9-inch pie pan

Filling

> 2 large eggs
> ½ cup granulated sugar
> ¼ cup cornstarch
> ¼ teaspoon salt
> 1 13.5-oz. can coconut milk
> Whole milk to make 2 cups of liquid with coconut milk
> 1 tablespoon unsalted butter
> 1 teaspoon pure vanilla extract
> 1 teaspoon pure coconut extract

Topping

> ¾ cup heavy cream
> 2 tablespoons confectioner's sugar
> 1½ teaspoons pure vanilla extract
> ¼ cup toasted sweetened flaked coconut*

* Spread sweetened flaked coconut in a thin layer on a small baking tray. Bake in preheated 350°F oven, stirring every few minutes until light golden brown. This will only take a few minutes. Don't leave the oven!

To make Filling:

1. Beat eggs in large bowl of electric mixer at medium-high speed until foamy. Gradually add sugar a little at a time and continue beating until the mixture is pale yellow and thick. Add cornstarch and salt and beat until well blended.

2. Bring coconut milk and whole milk (total 2 cups liquid) to a boil in a large, heavy saucepan over medium-high heat while you are beating the eggs.

3. With the mixer on low, gradually add hot milk mixture to egg mixture in a thin stream. Quickly scrape sides and bottom of bowl and mix at medium speed until well blended.

4. Pour the custard mixture back into the saucepan and cook it over medium-high heat, stirring constantly with a wire whip, until it comes to a boil and thickens. Lower heat and cook for 1 minute more. Remove from heat and beat in butter, vanilla, and coconut extract.

5. Put custard into medium bowl or plastic container to cool. Cover with plastic wrap to prevent skin from forming over the surface and chill in refrigerator. *Can be stored in refrigerator for up to 5 days or in freezer for up to 1 month in a tightly sealed container. Keep plastic wrap on surface.*

6. Pour cooled coconut custard into cooled prebaked Tart Shell Crust or Traditional Pie Crust.

To make Topping:

7. Combine heavy cream, confectioner's sugar, and vanilla in large bowl of electric mixer; beat until stiff peaks form. Use pastry bag to pipe sweetened heavy cream around edges of pie. Sprinkle toasted coconut over top of whipped cream. Refrigerate until well chilled. Serve cold.

Store in refrigerator. Best when eaten within 3 days of baking.

VANILLA CREAM PIE FILLING

Makes about 2 ¹/₂ cups

You can use this simple, delicious vanilla custard in a wide variety of desserts. It has a dense, creamy texture and a rich vanilla flavor. The recipe is relatively simply: Just follow the step-by-step instructions and you'll have fabulous results each time you make it. This custard is my filling of choice for Fresh Berry Fruit Tarts, Boston Cream Pie, and Banana Cream Pie (see recipes below).

> 4 large egg yolks
> ²/₃ cup granulated sugar
> ¹/₄ cup cornstarch
> ¹/₄ teaspoon salt
> 2 cups whole milk
> 1 tablespoon unsalted butter
> 2 tablespoons vanilla extract

Can be stored in refrigerator for up to 5 days or in freezer for up to 1 month in a tightly sealed container. Keep plastic wrap directly on surface of custard.

1. Beat egg yolks in large bowl of electric mixer at medium-high speed until foamy. Gradually add sugar a little at a time and continue beating until the mixture is pale yellow and thick. Add cornstarch and salt and beat until well blended.

2. Bring milk to a boil in a large, heavy saucepan over medium-high heat while you are beating the egg yolks.

3. With the mixer on low, gradually add hot milk to egg mixture in a thin stream. Quickly scrape sides and bottom of bowl and mix at medium speed until well blended.

4. Pour the custard mixture back into the saucepan and cook it over a medium-high heat, stirring constantly with a wire whip, until it comes to a boil and thickens. Lower heat and cook for 1 minute more. Remove from heat and beat in butter and vanilla.

5. Put custard in medium bowl or plastic container to cool. Cover with plastic wrap to prevent a skim from forming over surface and chill in refrigerator.

FRESH BERRY FRUIT TARTS

Spread cooled Vanilla Cream Pie Filling into cooled prebaked Traditional Pie Crust (see pp. 71, 72) or Tart Shell Crust (see p. 73). Arrange 1 1/2–2 cups fresh strawberries, blueberries, and/or raspberries (rinsed and completely dry) on top of custard.

Place 1/2 cup strawberry jelly and 1 tablespoon brandy or cognac in small saucepan and simmer until jelly is dissolved and liquefied but thickened slightly. Carefully brush onto berries. Refrigerate until ready to serve.

Store in refrigerator. Best when eaten within 3 days of baking.

BOSTON CREAM PIE

Use a long, thin knife to slice a cooled 8- or 9-inch round of vanilla layer cake horizontally in half (use Vanilla Cupcakes recipe, p. 36, and follow instructions to make 8- or 9-inch cake round). Spread about half the cooled Vanilla Cream Pie Filling across bottom cake half (consider making only half the recipe unless you want some leftover). Replace top half of cake.

Spread Chocolate Glaze (recipe follows) evenly across top layer of cake. Chill until chocolate has set.

Store in refrigerator. Best when eaten within 3 days of baking.

Chocolate Glaze

Melt 6 ounces semisweet chocolate and 4 tablespoons unsalted butter in a small, heavy saucepan over medium-low heat; stir constantly until smooth. Immediately remove from heat.

BANANA CREAM PIE

Cut 2 large ripe bananas into 1/4-inch-thick slices and mix into cooled Vanilla Cream Pie Filling. Spread into cooled prebaked Traditional Pie Crust (see pp. 71, 72) or Tart Shell Crust (see p. 73). Pipe Whipped Cream Topping (recipe follows) around outer rim of pie and chill until very cold.

Store in refrigerator. Best when eaten within 3 days of baking.

Whipped Cream Topping

Combine 3/4 cup heavy cream, 2 tablespoons confectioner's sugar, and 1 1/2 teaspoons vanilla in large bowl of electric mixer; beat until stiff peaks form. Use pastry bag to pipe sweetened heavy cream around edges of pie.

CHAPTER 7

Cookies

WE ALL HAVE FAVORITE COOKIES that we can't resist. They make our mouths water, remind us of holidays or special family members, and bring comfort and happiness. Fortunately for the gluten-intolerant, cookies are relatively easy to make gluten-free. In fact, many are actually better without wheat. You will find easy success in this chapter. The recipes are very basic and simple to master. In fact, if you are a baking novice, I suggest you start with a cookie recipe. It's hard to go wrong.

If you have a well-stocked pantry (see Chapter 3), you'll be able to make any of these recipes at a moment's notice. You'll also find suggestions for freezing dough because I think having easy access to pre-made cookie dough is a luxury worth having. You can bake a fresh batch of cookies for after-school snacks or a special after-dinner treat without starting from scratch.

During the holidays, I usually have at least three cookie doughs in my freezer, fewer during the rest of the year. The only trick you may want to fine tune is making a smooth log of cookie dough to slice. Many of the recipes here call for shaping the dough into a log so that you can easily slice the cookies. After you put the dough in the refrigerator or freezer to chill, take it out and reshape the log after about 15 minutes to make sure it does not flatten out.

CHOCOLATE CHIP COOKIES

CREAM-FILLED CHOCOLATE COOKIES

BUTTER COOKIES
Cream-Filled Butter Cookies
Chocolate-Filled Butter Cookies

SUGAR COOKIES

SHORTBREAD COOKIES
Coconut
Lemon
Lemon Cornmeal

CHOCOLATE SHORTBREAD COOKIES

LINZERTORTE COOKIES

ALMOND BUTTER COOKIES

PECAN BUTTER COOKIES

COCONUT MACAROONS

GINGERSNAPS

OATMEAL COOKIES

ALMOND BISCOTTI

HAZELNUT BISCOTTI

CHOCOLATE PEANUT BUTTER BALLS

Have you ever noticed that sometimes when you make a cookie recipe, the cookies turn out crisp and high, and the next time you make the same cookie recipe with exactly the same ingredients, the cookies are flat and chewy? The difference is due to the temperature of the ingredients—particularly the fats. If you use cold butter or shortening, your cookies will not spread as much, will take longer to bake, and will be crisper (though not necessarily crisp). In fact, we purposely chill the dough when we make shortbreads. If you use room-temperature butter or shortening, especially if the room is warm, your cookies will spread more, take less time to bake, and be chewier.

This chapter uses the following pans:
• Large, heavy baking sheets or cookie trays

THE LAST WORD ON COOKIES
• Set-up before starting the recipe: assemble all the ingredients

• Measure carefully (see Chapter 3)

• Preheat the oven to the proper temperature (make sure the oven is calibrated correctly)

• Do not open the oven door more than necessary

• Use a timer because you can get distracted. Test for doneness at the first time given in the recipe, then continue baking, if necessary, until the cookie is fully cooked. Make a note of the total baking time for the next time you make the recipe

CHOCOLATE CHIP COOKIES

This is the very first recipe I converted to gluten-free. I was hungry for these cookies for more than a year before I actually tried to make them without wheat. Six months later, when we found out one of my sons could no longer eat gluten, making them became a necessity: these had been his favorite cookies.

Take note: The recipe calls for vegetable shortening (yes, you can use the new shortenings made without trans fats); if you use butter, the dough will spread all over the cookie sheet.

I usually make up a batch of dough, bake one sheet, and then freeze the rest of the dough in two small, tightly sealed containers. If you want to make chocolate chip cookie dough ice cream, make a half recipe, using a pasteurized egg substitute to make the dough. Then roll it into tiny pieces, freeze it, and add it to your ice cream maker as instructed.

> 1 cup vegetable shortening (not butter or margarine)
>
> 1 cup granulated sugar
>
> ½ cup dark brown sugar
>
> 2 large eggs
>
> 1 tablespoon pure vanilla extract
>
> 2 cups plus 2 tablespoons Brown Rice Flour Mix (see p. 6)
>
> 1½ teaspoons baking soda
>
> 1 teaspoon xanthan gum
>
> ½ teaspoon salt
>
> 12 ozs. chocolate chips (optional: plus ¼ cup)
>
> 1 cup chopped nuts (optional)

1. Preheat oven to 375° F. Position rack in center of oven. Lightly grease cookie sheet with cooking spray.

2. Beat shortening and both sugars at medium speed in large bowl of electric mixer. Add eggs and vanilla; beat until fluffy.

3. Add flour, baking soda, xanthan gum, and salt; mix at medium speed until well blended. Mix in chocolate chips and nuts.

4. Drop heaping teaspoons of dough onto cookie sheet 2 inches apart. Bake in center of oven for 8–10 minutes until light golden brown. (For convection ovens, bake at 350°F using no more than 3 trays at a time.) Transfer to a wire rack and cool. Store in an airtight container.

Makes about 70 cookies. Recipe can be cut in half

Best when eaten within 3 days of baking. After 3 days, store in refrigerator. Can be kept in refrigerator for 2 weeks or frozen for up to 1 month.

Unbaked dough can be kept in refrigerator for up to 3 days in tightly sealed plastic container or frozen for up to 1 month. To freeze, cover top of dough with plastic wrap and place inside tightly sealed plastic container so no air touches dough.

CREAM-FILLED CHOCOLATE COOKIES

Makes about 40 filled cookies or 80 single cookies

This cookie does not really try to replace the store-bought version we all know and remember. It has more real chocolate flavor and tastes fresher. The cream filling does, however, try to give the kids on my cookie-testing panels what they want and expect in a cream-filled cookie: the sweet, shortening-based filling that kids everywhere seem to love (you can use the new shortenings made without trans fats). I tried fancy real cream fillings and buttercreams, but no, the cream filling below was the winner. Of course, you *could* use a more grown-up filling, but then the little kid in *you* might squawk.

Unbaked dough can be stored in refrigerator for up to 3 days or frozen for up to 2 months. To freeze, wrap plastic-wrapped log of dough in foil.

- ³⁄₄ cup unsalted butter
- 1 cup granulated sugar
- 1 large egg
- 1 teaspoon pure vanilla extract
- 1³⁄₄ cups Brown Rice Flour Mix (see p. 6)
- ¹⁄₄ cup sweet rice flour
- ¹⁄₂ cup baking cocoa
- 1 teaspoon baking powder
- 1 teaspoon baking soda
- 1 teaspoon xanthan gum
- ¹⁄₄ teaspoon salt

Cream Filling

- 3 tablespoons vegetable shortening
- 2 cups confectioner's sugar
- ³⁄₄ teaspoon pure vanilla extract
- 2 tablespoons hot water

1. Beat butter and sugar at medium speed in large bowl of electric mixer until light and creamy. Add egg and vanilla and beat well.

2. Add flours, baking cocoa, baking powder, baking soda, xanthan gum, and salt; mix until a soft, smooth dough is formed.

3. Divide dough into two equal halves. Drop first half in small mounds across a large sheet of plastic wrap. Fold the plastic over the dough and shape into a long, 1-inch-diameter log, leaving plastic open at the ends. Twist ends and flatten dough at each end. Try to smooth log by rolling back and forth on counter. Repeat with second half of dough. Refrigerate both rolls until well chilled.

4. Preheat oven to 350°F. Position rack in center of oven. Lightly grease cookie sheet with cooking spray.

5. Using a thin, sharp knife, slice chilled dough into $\frac{1}{8}$-inch slices and place 1 inch apart on cookie sheet. Bake in center of oven for about 9 minutes or until cooked through. Cool slightly on cookie sheet and transfer to wire rack to cool completely.

To make Cream Filling:

6. Combine shortening, confectioner's sugar, vanilla, and hot water in large bowl of electric mixer. Beat until light and creamy. Spread filling on one side of a cookie and cover with another cookie. Store in airtight container.

After 3 days, store cookies in refrigerator. Can be kept in refrigerator for 2 weeks or frozen for up to 1 month.

BUTTER COOKIES

*Makes about
40 cookies.
Recipe can be doubled*

One day I started to crave the kind of tender, flavorful butter cookies they sell at good bakeries. Recreating them proved to be a bit of a challenge, but the end result is this classic butter cookie with an excellent melt-in-your-mouth texture and taste. Dress them up with candied cherries, dip them in chocolate and sprinkles, or make sandwich cookies by spreading the Cream Filling or Chocolate Filling (recipes follow) between two cookies and pressing them together. For effortless variety, try jam, lemon curd, or prepared frostings. You can also use this recipe to make cut-out or spritz butter cookies to decorate for holidays.

$\frac{1}{2}$ cup unsalted butter

$\frac{1}{3}$ cup granulated sugar

1 large egg

$1\frac{1}{2}$ teaspoons pure vanilla extract

1 cup Brown Rice Flour Mix (see p. 6)

$\frac{1}{4}$ teaspoon baking powder

$\frac{1}{4}$ teaspoon xanthan gum

$\frac{1}{8}$ teaspoon salt

Unbaked dough can be stored in refrigerator for up to 1 week or frozen for up to 2 months. To freeze, wrap logs in plastic wrap and then wrap in foil.

After 3 days, store cookies in refrigerator. Can be kept in refrigerator for 2 weeks or frozen for up to 1 month.

1. Preheat oven to 325°F. Position rack in center of oven. Lightly grease cookie sheet with cooking spray.

2. Beat butter and sugar together in large bowl of electric mixer until light and creamy. Add egg and vanilla and mix until smooth.

3. Add flour, baking powder, xanthan gum, and salt; beat at medium-high speed until a soft, smooth dough is formed.

4. Shape dough into a flat square and wrap in wax paper; refrigerate for 30 minutes. Drop half of dough in small mounds across a large sheet of plastic wrap. Fold the plastic over the dough and shape into a long, 1-inch-diameter log, leaving plastic open at the ends. Twist ends and flatten dough at each end. Try to smooth log by rolling back and forth on counter. Repeat with second half of dough. Refrigerate both rolls until well chilled. *For spritz cookies: Chill until cold.*

5. Using a thin, sharp knife, slice chilled dough into $\frac{1}{4}$-inch slices and place 1 inch apart on cookie sheet. Top with granulated sugar, colored sprinkles, candied cherries, or mini chocolate morsels, if desired. Bake in center of oven for 12–15 minutes or until a very light golden color. Bottom should be light golden brown. Transfer to a wire rack and cool. Store in an airtight container.

CREAM-FILLED BUTTER COOKIES

Cream Filling

    3 tablespoons vegetable shortening

    2 cups confectioner's sugar

    $\frac{3}{4}$ teaspoon vanilla

    2 tablespoons hot water

1. Combine shortening, confectioner's sugar, vanilla, and hot water in large bowl of electric mixer. Beat until light and creamy. Spread filling on one side of a cookie and cover with another cookie. Store in airtight container.

After 3 days, store cookies in refrigerator. Can be kept in refrigerator for 2 weeks or frozen for up to 1 month.

CHOCOLATE-FILLED BUTTER COOKIES

Chocolate Filling

    3 ozs. semisweet chocolate, chopped

    1 teaspoon canola oil

1. Combine chopped chocolate and canola oil in a small, heavy saucepan. Melt chocolate over a low heat, stirring constantly. Remove from heat. Spread filling on one side of a cookie and cover with another cookie. Store in airtight container.

After 3 days, store cookies in refrigerator. Can be kept in refrigerator for 2 weeks or frozen for up to 1 month.

SUGAR COOKIES

*Makes about
80 cookies*

These sugar cookies are light, crunchy, sweet, and delicious—just like sugar cookies are supposed to be. In fact, they passed the kid testing panel with flying colors. They are perfect just the way they are, or you can dress them up with sprinkles or colored icings for the holidays. The sweet rice flour is necessary to help give them the body they need to pass the sugar cookie-criterion test set by my panel of experts: crunchy yet chewy. The dough freezes well and is ideal to keep on hand for snacks or school lunches.

$\frac{3}{4}$ cup unsalted butter

1 cup granulated sugar

1 large egg

1 tablespoon pure vanilla extract

$1\frac{3}{4}$ cups Brown Rice Flour Mix (see p. 6)

$\frac{1}{4}$ cup sweet rice flour

1 teaspoon baking powder

1 teaspoon xanthan gum

$\frac{1}{4}$ teaspoon salt

Unbaked dough can be stored in refrigerator for up to 1 week or frozen for up to 2 months. To freeze, wrap logs in plastic wrap and then wrap in foil.

After 3 days, store cookies in refrigerator. Can be kept in refrigerator for 2 weeks or frozen for up to 1 month.

1. Beat butter and sugar in large bowl of electric mixer until light and creamy. Add egg and vanilla and mix until smooth.

2. Add flours, baking powder, xanthan gum, and salt; beat until a thick, smooth dough is formed.

3. Shape dough into a flat square and wrap in wax paper; refrigerate for 30 minutes. Drop half of dough in small mounds across a large sheet of plastic wrap. Fold the plastic over the dough and shape into a long, 1-inch-diameter log, leaving plastic open at the ends. Twist ends and flatten dough at each end. Try to smooth log by rolling back and forth on counter. Repeat with second half of dough. Refrigerate both rolls until well chilled.

4. Preheat oven to 350°F. Position rack in center of oven. Lightly grease cookie sheet with cooking spray.

5. Using a thin, sharp knife, slice chilled dough into $\frac{1}{4}$-inch slices and place 1 inch apart on cookie sheet. Bake in center of oven for 12–15 minutes or until a very light golden color. Transfer to a wire rack and cool. Store in an airtight container.

For cutout cookies: Roll out dough between 2 large sheets of wax paper. Chill until very cold. Cut into desired shapes with cookie cutters, and chill again on cookie sheet before baking.

SHORTBREAD COOKIES

The original recipe for these shortbreads was a family favorite. I often used the dough to make cut-out cookies for holidays: little Christmas trees with red or green sprinkles in December, colorful Easter eggs in the spring, tiny orange pumpkins in the fall, delicate hearts with red sprinkles for Valentine's Day. I made them year 'round even when there were no holidays because my children loved them. Fortunately, they are still a favorite in their new gluten-free version.

You can make these shortbreads in my easy roll-and-slice version, pat them into traditional rounds and cut them into pie-shaped wedges, or use a cookie cutter to cut them into special shapes. No matter which method you choose, you'll have a great-tasting classic shortbread that will keep you coming back for more. Try the coconut, lemon, and lemon cornmeal versions, too, for a really special treat (recipes follow).

$\frac{1}{2}$ cup unsalted butter

$\frac{1}{4}$ cup granulated sugar

$1\frac{1}{2}$ teaspoons pure vanilla extract

$\frac{3}{4}$ cup Brown Rice Flour Mix (see p. 6)

$\frac{1}{4}$ cup sweet rice flour

$\frac{1}{4}$ teaspoon xanthan gum

$\frac{1}{8}$ teaspoon salt

Granulated sugar

1. Beat butter and sugar in large bowl of electric mixer until light and creamy. Add vanilla and mix well.

2. Add flours, xanthan gum, and salt; mix until a soft dough is formed.

3. Drop dough in small mounds across a large sheet of plastic wrap. Fold the plastic over the dough and shape into a long, 1-inch-diameter log, leaving plastic open at the ends. Twist ends and flatten dough at each end. Try to smooth log by rolling back and forth on counter. Refrigerate until well chilled.

4. Preheat oven to 350°F. Position rack in center of oven. Lightly grease cookie sheet with cooking spray.

5. Using a thin, sharp knife, slice chilled dough into $\frac{5}{8}$-inch slices and place on greased cookie sheet 1 inch apart. Sprinkle with granulated sugar. Chill cookies (on cookie sheet) until cold before baking. Bake in center of oven for 12–14 minutes or until light golden. Cookies should not brown. Cool slightly on cookie sheet and transfer to wire rack to cool completely. Store in an airtight container.

*Makes about
30 cookies.
Recipe can be doubled*

Unbaked dough can be stored in refrigerator for up to 1 week or frozen for up to 2 months. To freeze, wrap plastic-wrapped log of dough in foil.

After 3 days, store cookies in refrigerator. Can be kept in refrigerator for 2 weeks or frozen for up to 1 month.

Alternate shape: Pat dough into two 6-inch rounds, about ½ inch thick, on cookie sheet. Sprinkle with granulated sugar. Crimp edges decoratively and prick top of dough with tines of fork. Lightly score circle of dough into 6 triangles; do not push knife completely through dough. Bake about 15 minutes until light golden and centers are cooked. Cookies should not brown. Cut out triangles with a sharp knife while still warm.

For cutout cookies: Roll out dough between 2 large sheets of wax paper. Chill until very cold. Cut into desired shapes with cookie cutters, and chill again on cookie sheet before baking.

COCONUT SHORTBREAD COOKIES

In Step 2 add ¼ cup shredded sweetened coconut that was pulverized in a food processor or blender, and ½ teaspoon coconut extract.

LEMON SHORTBREAD COOKIES

In Step 2, add 1 teaspoon (packed) grated lemon rind, and ½ teaspoon lemon extract.

LEMON CORNMEAL SHORTBREAD COOKIES

In Step 2, add 1 teaspoon (packed) grated lemon rind, and ½ teaspoon lemon extract, and substitute ¼ cup cornmeal for ¼ cup of the Brown Rice Flour Mix.

CHOCOLATE SHORTBREAD COOKIES

*Makes about
40 cookies.
Recipe can be doubled*

This is an exquisite, melt-in-your-mouth shortbread cookie that children of all ages will love. The rich chocolate flavor is perfect with milk or special after-dinner coffees. The dough mixes up quickly and freezes well. I usually make a double batch and freeze several small rolls to use in later weeks.

$\frac{1}{2}$ cup unsalted butter

$\frac{1}{4}$ cup granulated sugar

1 teaspoon pure vanilla extract

$\frac{3}{4}$ cup Brown Rice Flour Mix (see p. 6)

2 tablespoons sweet rice flour

$\frac{1}{4}$ cup cocoa powder

$\frac{1}{4}$ teaspoon xanthan gum

$\frac{1}{8}$ teaspoon salt

$\frac{1}{2}$ cup semisweet mini chocolate chips

Granulated sugar

1. Beat butter and sugar in large bowl of electric mixer until light and creamy. Add vanilla and mix well.

2. Add flours, cocoa powder, xanthan gum, and salt; mix until a soft dough is formed. Mix in chocolate chips.

3. Shape dough into a flat square and wrap in wax paper; refrigerate for 30 minutes. Drop dough in small mounds across a large sheet of plastic wrap. Fold the plastic over the dough and shape into a long, 1-inch-diameter log, leaving plastic open at the ends. Twist ends and flatten dough at each end. Try to smooth log by rolling back and forth on counter. Refrigerate until well chilled.

4. Preheat oven to 350°F. Position rack in center of oven. Lightly grease cookie sheet with cooking spray.

5. Using a thin, sharp knife, slice chilled dough into $\frac{5}{8}$-inch slices and place on greased cookie sheet 1 inch apart. Sprinkle with granulated sugar. Chill cookies (on cookie sheet) until cold before baking. Bake in center of oven for 8–10 minutes or until centers are cooked. Cool slightly on cookie sheet and transfer to wire rack to cool completely. Store in an airtight container.

Unbaked dough can be stored in refrigerator for up to 1 week or frozen for up to 2 months. To freeze, wrap plastic-wrapped log of dough in foil.

After 3 days, store cookies in refrigerator. Can be kept in refrigerator for 2 weeks or frozen for up to 1 month.

Alternate shape: Pat dough into two 6-inch rounds, about ½ inch thick, on cookie sheet. Sprinkle with granulated sugar. Crimp edges decoratively and prick top of dough with tines of fork. Lightly score circle of dough into 6 triangles, but do not push knife through dough. Bake 12–14 minutes or until centers are cooked. Cut triangles out with a sharp knife while still warm.

LINZERTORTE COOKIES

These were the most difficult of all the cookies to convert to gluten-free. I tried unsuccessfully for two Christmases to get Linzertorte connoisseur Carl Scariati to give me his seal of approval. I had made them for decades in their fabulous original form, and that was a hard act to follow. The texture is supposed to be light yet rich, crumbly but firm, delicate enough to melt in your mouth yet with enough staying power to blend with the raspberry preserves. Finally, I developed a gluten-free version that made Carl smile, and I am proud to include it in this book.

*Makes about
40 filled cookies
or 80 single cookies*

1 cup unsalted butter

²⁄₃ cup confectioner's sugar

3 tablespoons well-beaten large egg

1½ cups Brown Rice Flour Mix (see p. 6)

½ cup sweet rice flour

½ teaspoon xanthan gum

1⅓ cups finely ground walnuts

½ cup seedless red raspberry preserves

Confectioner's sugar

Unbaked dough can be stored in refrigerator for up to 1 week or frozen for up to 2 months. To freeze, shape dough into a flattened round; wrap in plastic wrap and then wrap in foil.

After 3 days, store cookies in refrigerator. Can be kept in refrigerator for 2 weeks or frozen for up to 1 month.

1. Beat butter and sugar in large bowl of electric mixer until light and fluffy. Add egg and mix until smooth.

2. Add flours and xanthan gum; beat until a smooth dough is formed. Mix in walnuts.

3. Roll dough ¼ inch thick between two large sheets of wax paper. Chill until very cold. Cut into desired shapes with 1 ½-inch cookie cutters. Chill cookies (on cookie sheet) until cold before baking.

4. Preheat oven to 325°F. Position rack in center of oven. Lightly grease cookie sheet with cooking spray.

5. Bake in center of oven for 12–14 minutes or until a very light golden color. Test for doneness. Bottom should be golden. Transfer to a wire rack and cool. Store unfilled cookies in an airtight container.

6. Within 4 hours of serving, spread half of the cookies you plan on using with ½ teaspoon of raspberry preserves. Top with remaining cookies. Sift confectioner's sugar over all completed cookies. Store any uneaten filled cookies in refrigerator. *For best texture, it is best to fill them within 4 hours of serving.*

ALMOND BUTTER COOKIES

Makes about
60 cookies.
Recipe can be
cut in half

These luscious butter cookies have a rich almond flavor and a firm texture. I made the original recipe for years at Christmas time because they reminded me of a cookie made with almond paste that my grandparents would bring me when I was a child. Now in their gluten-free form, they are great for the holidays or any time you yearn for something a little special. Both the dough and the cookies freeze exceptionally well.

$3\frac{1}{2}$ ozs. almond paste

$\frac{1}{2}$ cup granulated sugar

2 large egg yolks

$\frac{1}{2}$ teaspoon almond extract

$\frac{3}{4}$ cup unsalted butter

2 cups Brown Rice Flour Mix (see p. 6)

$\frac{1}{2}$ teaspoon xanthan gum

$\frac{2}{3}$ cup finely chopped almonds

Confectioner's sugar

Unbaked dough can be kept in refrigerator for up to 3 days in tightly sealed plastic container or frozen for up to 1 month. To freeze, cover top of dough with plastic wrap and place inside tightly sealed plastic container so no air touches dough.

After 3 days, store cookies in refrigerator. Can be kept in refrigerator for 2 weeks or frozen for up to 1 month.

1. Preheat oven to 350°F. Position rack in center of oven. Lightly grease cookie sheet with cooking spray.

2. Beat almond paste, sugar, egg yolks, and almond extract in large bowl of electric mixer for 3 minutes or until almond paste is thoroughly incorporated and smooth. Add butter and beat until light and fluffy.

3. Add flour and xanthan gum; beat until a smooth dough is formed. Mix in almonds.

4. Use your hands to shape dough into $\frac{3}{4}$-inch balls, crescents, or ovals and place on cookie sheet.

5. Bake in center of oven for 12–14 minutes or until a very light golden color. Test for doneness. Bottom should be light golden brown. Transfer to a wire rack and cool. Sprinkle with confectioner's sugar. Store in an airtight container.

PECAN BUTTER COOKIES

Perhaps you have missed the taste and texture of those delicate pecan-based cookies called Mexican Wedding Cakes. The cookie has other names as well, including pecan sandies and pecan meltaways. But no mater what you call it, it is a recipe that converts well to gluten-free. This buttery cookie is chock full of sweet nutty pecans. It's great for holiday cookie trays, afternoon snacks with iced tea and lemonade, or anytime you want a tender, delicious cookie.

> 1 cup unsalted butter
>
> 6 tablespoons confectioner's sugar
>
> 2 teaspoons pure vanilla extract
>
> 2 cups Brown Rice Flour Mix (see p. 6)
>
> 1 teaspoon xanthan gum
>
> 1 cup pecans, toasted and chopped*
>
> Confectioner's sugar

1. Preheat oven to 350°F. Position rack in center of oven. Lightly grease cookie sheet with cooking spray.

2. Beat butter and sugar in large bowl of electric mixer until light and creamy. Add vanilla and mix until smooth.

3. Add flour and xanthan gum; beat until a smooth dough is formed. Mix in pecans.

4. Use your hands to shape dough into 1-inch balls. Roll balls in confectioner's sugar and place on cookie sheet.

5. Bake in center of oven for 12–15 minutes or until a very light golden color. Test for doneness. Bottom should be light golden brown. Transfer to a wire rack and cool. Store in an airtight container.

Makes about 50 cookies. Recipe can be cut in half

Unbaked dough can be kept in refrigerator for up to 3 days in tightly sealed plastic container or frozen for up to 1 month. To freeze, cover top of dough with plastic wrap and place inside tightly sealed plastic container so no air touches dough.

After 3 days, store cookies in refrigerator. Can be kept in refrigerator for 2 weeks or frozen for up to 1 month.

* Bake pecans about 5 minutes in preheated 350°F oven.

COCONUT MACAROONS

*Makes about
20 cookies.
Recipe can be doubled*

Everyone who loves macaroons seems to have a favorite recipe. My family had been making this one in its original form for years, and it was a treasured Christmas cookie. Fortunately, it was really easy to convert to gluten-free. In fact, no one was able to tell the first year I made the switch. Be sure you mix the cream of coconut well before you measure it (you can freeze the rest to use another time).

2 7-oz. packages sweetened flaked coconut

²⁄₃ cup confectioner's sugar

¹⁄₄ cup canned cream of coconut

1 oz. cream cheese

3 tablespoons Brown Rice Flour Mix (see p. 6)

1 large egg white

1 teaspoon pure vanilla extract

Pinch of salt

After 3 days, store cookies in refrigerator. Can be kept in refrigerator for 2 weeks or frozen for up to 1 month.

1. Preheat oven to 325°F. Position rack in center of oven. Line cookie sheet with heavy foil and spray lightly with cooking spray.

2. Chop contents of one 7-ounce bag of coconut with confectioner's sugar in food processor for 1 minute.

3. Add cream of coconut, cream cheese, flour, egg white, vanilla, and salt; process until a soft dough is formed.

4. Place balance of coconut in a soup bowl. Drop rounded teaspoons of dough into coconut and roll to coat completely; drop onto cookie sheet 2 inches apart. Bake in center of oven for about 20 minutes or until golden. Transfer to wire rack and cool. Store in airtight container.

GINGERSNAPS

There's something about a spicy gingersnap cookie and a cup of fragrant, hot mulled cider that shouts Christmas. Come the beginning of December and the first sightings of Santa hats in the stores, visions of sugar and spice blend with distant strains of *The Nutcracker Suite* to get me in the mood for the holidays. But, of course, these gingersnaps are good any time you'd like to add a little spice to your day. Fast and easy to make, they are a great cookie to keep in the refrigerator or freezer because they stay fresh for a long time. The dough also freezes well, so you can bake a fresh batch anytime you want.

Makes about 56 cookies

- ¾ cup vegetable shortening
- 1 cup granulated sugar
- 1 large egg
- ¼ cup molasses
- 1¾ cups Brown Rice Flour Mix (see p. 6)
- ¼ cup sweet rice flour
- 2 teaspoons baking soda
- ½ teaspoon xanthan gum
- 1 teaspoon cinnamon
- ¾ teaspoon ground ginger
- ¼ teaspoon ground cloves
- ¼ teaspoon salt
- Confectioner's sugar

1. Beat shortening and sugar in large bowl of electric mixer until light and creamy. Beat in egg and molasses and mix until smooth.

2. Add flours, baking soda, xanthan gum, cinnamon, ginger, cloves, and salt; mix to form a soft dough. Shape dough into a flat square and wrap in plastic wrap. Refrigerate for 30 minutes.

3. Preheat oven to 375°F. Position rack in center of oven. Lightly grease cookie sheet with cooking spray.

4. Use your hands to shape dough into 1-inch balls. Roll balls in confectioner's sugar and place on cookie sheet.

5. Bake 8–10 minutes or until cooked through. Transfer to a wire rack and cool. Store in an airtight container.

Unbaked dough can be kept in refrigerator for up to 3 days in tightly sealed plastic container or frozen for up to 1 month. To freeze, cover top of dough with plastic wrap and place inside tightly sealed plastic container so no air touches dough.

After 3 days, store cookies in refrigerator. Can be kept in refrigerator for 2 weeks or frozen for up to 1 month.

OATMEAL COOKIES
(WITH OR WITHOUT OATMEAL)

Makes about
60 cookies.
Recipe can be
cut in half

These delicious cookies are laced with cinnamon, nutmeg, and ginger. If you use butter, they will be somewhat chewy; shortening makes a crisper version (yes, you can use the new shortenings without trans fats).

Although there is concern in the gluten-free community about our ability to buy uncontaminated oats, it appears that McCann's® Irish Oatmeal offers a product we can trust. But if you are hungry for the taste of oatmeal cookies and still not convinced, you can make this recipe without oats by using a soy flake product made by Bob's Red Mill.® Take note: the soy flavor comes through more strongly once the cookies are several days old. You may want to bake a small batch and then freeze the dough to bake another time; that way you will be able to have fresh cookies without the strong soy taste.

Unbaked dough can be kept in refrigerator for up to 3 days in tightly sealed plastic container or frozen for up to 1 month. To freeze, cover top of dough with plastic wrap and place inside tightly sealed plastic container so no air touches dough.

After 3 days, store cookies in refrigerator. Can be kept in refrigerator for 2 weeks

1 cup unsalted butter *or* vegetable shortening

1 cup dark brown sugar

1 cup granulated sugar

2 large eggs

1 tablespoon pure vanilla extract

2 cups Brown Rice Flour Mix (see p. 6)

2 teaspoons baking powder

1 teaspoon baking soda

$^3/_4$ teaspoon xanthan gum

$^1/_2$ teaspoon salt

$^1/_2$ teaspoon cinnamon

$^1/_2$ teaspoon nutmeg

$^1/_2$ teaspoon ground ginger

2 cups McCann's® Quick Cooking Irish Oatmeal *or* Bob's Red Mill® Soy Flakes

1 cup raisins

1. Preheat oven to 350°F. Position rack in center of oven. Lightly grease cookie sheet with cooking spray.

2. Beat shortening and sugars in large bowl of electric mixer until light and creamy. Add eggs and vanilla and mix until smooth.

3. Add flour, baking powder, baking soda, xanthan gum, salt, cinnamon, nutmeg, and ginger; beat until a smooth dough is formed. Mix in oats (or soy flakes) and raisins.

4. Drop heaping teaspoons of dough onto cookie sheet. Bake in center of oven for about 10 minutes. Transfer to a wire rack and cool. Store in an airtight container.

ALMOND BISCOTTI

You will find different versions of this classic biscotti everywhere you go. I had a much-loved recipe and was worried I would never be able to make it again. Luckily, gluten-free flours make fabulous biscotti, and my recipe is even better now in its new gluten-free form. These biscotti are simple to make and keep amazingly well in the refrigerator or freezer. Make a batch once and you'll never want to be without them again.

Makes about 36 cookies

    2 cups Brown Rice Flour Mix (see p. 6)
    1 cup granulated sugar
    1 teaspoon baking powder
    1 teaspoon xanthan gum
    1/8 teaspoon salt
    2 large eggs
    1 tablespoon Amaretto
    2 teaspoons pure almond extract
    1 1/2 teaspoons pure vanilla extract
    1 teaspoon unsalted butter, room temperature
    3/4 cup whole almonds, lightly toasted and coarsely chopped*

1. Preheat oven to 300°F. Lightly grease and flour a large cookie sheet with cooking spray and rice flour.

2. Combine flour, sugar, baking powder, xanthan gum, and salt in large bowl of electric mixer. Add eggs, Amaretto, almond extract, vanilla, and butter; beat at medium speed until well combined. Mix in almonds. Dough will be very sticky and crumbly.

3. Use your hands to shape dough into two slightly flattened logs, each 8 inches long, 2 inches wide, and 1 inch high. Place logs 2 1/2 inches apart on cookie sheet.

4. Place in center of oven and bake 40–45 minutes or until light golden brown. Logs will spread and flatten. Remove to a cutting board and cool 8 minutes.

5. Using a cutting board and serrated knife, slice logs diagonally into 1/2-inch-wide biscotti. Place biscotti back on cookie sheet with the cut surfaces down and return to oven. Bake another 15–20 minutes or until golden brown. Turn biscotti over and bake another 12–15 minutes until golden brown on second side. Remove from oven and cool completely on a rack. Store in airtight container.

After 3 days, store cookies in refrigerator. Can be kept in refrigerator for 3 weeks or frozen for up to 6 weeks.

* Bake almonds about 6 minutes in preheated 350°F oven.

HAZELNUT BISCOTTI

*Makes about
36 cookies*

These crunchy biscotti are flavored with hazelnut liqueur and anise. They can be addictive, so you might find yourself keeping a small stash in your refrigerator or freezer. Grab one in the morning to go with your coffee, or serve them after dinner with a luscious dessert wine. They are easy to make; just follow the directions. And keep a bottle of Frangelico and some hazelnuts in your pantry so you can make them whenever your supply runs out.

> 2 cups Brown Rice Flour Mix (see p. 6)
> 1 cup granulated sugar
> 1$\frac{1}{4}$ teaspoons baking powder
> 1 teaspoon xanthan gum
> 2 large eggs
> 3 tablespoons Frangelico liqueur
> 1$\frac{1}{2}$ teaspoons pure vanilla extract
> 1$\frac{1}{2}$ teaspoons pure anise extract
> 1 cup whole hazelnuts, lightly toasted, skins removed, and coarsely chopped*

After 3 days, store cookies in refrigerator. Can be kept in refrigerator for 3 weeks or frozen for up to 6 weeks.

* Bake hazelnuts about 6 minutes in preheated 350°F oven. Skins are more easily removed after baking.

1. Preheat oven to 300°F. Position rack in center of oven. Lightly grease a large cookie sheet with cooking spray and dust with rice flour.

2. Combine flour, sugar, baking powder, and xanthan gum in large bowl of electric mixer. Add eggs, Frangelico, vanilla, and anise extract; beat at medium speed until well combined. Mix in hazelnuts. Dough will be thick.

3. Use your hands to shape dough into two slightly flattened logs, each 10 inches long, 3 inches wide, and $\frac{1}{2}$ inch high. Place logs 2$\frac{1}{2}$ inches apart on cookie sheet.

4. Place in center of oven and bake 40 minutes or until light, firm, and dry. Logs will spread slightly. Remove from oven and cool 8 minutes.

5. Using a cutting board and serrated knife, slice logs diagonally into $\frac{1}{2}$-inch-wide biscotti. Place biscotti back on cookie sheet with the cut surfaces down and return to oven. Bake another 15–20 minutes or until golden brown. Turn biscotti over and bake another 15–20 minutes. Remove from oven and cool completely on rack. Store in airtight container.

CHOCOLATE PEANUT BUTTER BALLS

If you like chocolate and peanut butter, these are probably the most addictive cookies on the planet. Family friend Diane Gillooly brought them each year to our annual Christmas caroling party. People would actually wait for her to arrive and then descend on her offering like locusts. I finally asked for the recipe so I could make it gluten-free for my family. I still only make Chocolate Peanut Butter Balls for the holidays, but we think about them throughout the year. Try them and you'll see why.

$\frac{1}{2}$ cup unsalted butter

18 ozs. smooth peanut butter

$3\frac{1}{2}$ cups confectioner's sugar

$2\frac{1}{2}$ cups gluten-free crispy rice cereal*

16 ozs. semisweet chocolate, chopped

1. Mix butter, peanut butter, and sugar together in large mixing bowl of electric mixer. Beat until creamy.

2. Add crispy rice cereal and mix until cereal is incorporated into dough. Chill until cold.

3. Form into 1-inch balls and refrigerate 12 hours. (It is easier to form balls if dough is chilled first.)

4. In a double boiler or microwave, melt chocolate and keep warm.

5. Dip balls in warm chocolate. Place on wax paper to cool. Refrigerate until chocolate hardens. Store in refrigerator in airtight container. Serve at room temperature or slightly chilled. Best when eaten within 1 week.

Makes about 72 cookies. Recipe can be cut in half

* There are currently very few gluten-free rice cereals, but Erewhon® Gluten Free Crispy Brown Rice Whole Grain Cereal is very good. Contact U.S. Mills, Inc., Erewhon, 200 Reservoir Street, Needham, MA 02494 (www.usmillsinc.com) to find a supplier.

Other Sweet Treats

THIS CHAPTER IS FILLED with a broad assortment of delectable treats. Some, like the brownies and fruit crisps, are so basic and simple that they might become a regular part of your baking routine. Others, like the eclairs and cream puffs, are a little more involved and might be saved for more special occasions. But no matter which recipe you choose, detailed, step-by-step instructions will allow you to try making things you might never have tried before.

Interestingly enough, many of the recipes here are actually better without wheat. The toppings on the fruit crisps and the crust of the lemon squares will stay firm and crunchy for days. No one will ever believe the brownies are gluten-free. And the ice cream sandwiches are so good, no one will care. Work your way through this chapter and try them all. The luscious bread puddings and fancy pastry cream puffs and eclairs will turn heads and become favorites.

This chapter uses the following pans:
- 9-inch deep-dish pie plate
- 9-inch round cake pan
- 8-inch square baking pan
- glass or ceramic 13 x 9 x 2-inch baking dish
- glass or ceramic 11 x 7 x 2-inch baking dish
- large, heavy baking sheet

THE LAST WORD ON SWEET TREATS

- Set-up before starting the recipe: assemble all the ingredients

- Measure carefully (see Chapter 3)

- Use an instant-read thermometer to check temperature of the puff paste dough for the cream puffs and eclairs

- Preheat the oven to the proper temperature (make sure the oven is calibrated correctly)

- Do not open the oven door more than necessary

- Use a timer because you can get distracted

BROWNIES

Once you make this recipe it will surely become a part of your gluten-free baking repertoire. My simple-to-make brownie is slightly chewy, slightly cake-like, and has a rich chocolate flavor. It keeps well in the refrigerator and freezes exceptionally well. It is perfect à la mode for dessert or by itself for school lunches and afternoon snacks.

Makes 16 brownies

- ²⁄₃ cup Brown Rice Flour Mix (see p. 6)
- ¹⁄₂ teaspoon salt
- ¹⁄₂ teaspoon baking powder
- ¹⁄₂ teaspoon xanthan gum
- 2 ozs. unsweetened chocolate
- 4 ozs. semisweet chocolate
- ¹⁄₂ cup unsalted butter
- 1¹⁄₄ cups granulated sugar
- 2 teaspoons pure vanilla extract
- 3 large eggs
- ³⁄₄ cup chopped toasted walnuts (optional)*

1. Preheat oven to 325°F. Position rack in lower-middle oven. Line bottom and sides of 8-inch square baking pan with foil and spray with cooking spray.

2. Combine flour, salt, baking powder, and xanthan gum in a small bowl. Set aside.

3. Melt chocolate and butter in a heavy, medium-size saucepan over low heat. Remove from heat; whisk in sugar and vanilla. Whisk in eggs, one at a time, and continue to whisk until mixture is completely smooth and glossy. Add flour mixture and whisk until just incorporated. Stir in nuts.

4. Pour batter into prepared pan and place in center of oven. Bake about 45 minutes or until a tester inserted into the center comes out with wet crumbs. Cool in pan on rack for 5 minutes. Remove brownies from pan by lifting out foil, and cool completely on rack. Cut into squares or triangles.

Brownies can be stored in refrigerator for up to 5 days or in freezer for 4 weeks; wrap in plastic wrap and then in foil.

* Bake walnuts about 5 minutes in preheated 350°F oven.

LEMON SQUARES

*Makes 16
lemon squares*

Light, luscious lemon squares are a favorite classic dessert. My gluten-free version has a melt-in-your-mouth crumbly crust and a tangy, not too sweet lemon filling. They are easy to make and disappear way too fast. Bake the lemon squares several hours ahead or the day before you plan on serving them in order to give them time to cool. They are perfect for a springtime picnic, dessert after a special dinner, or enjoy them with a cup of afternoon tea. No matter when you eat them, they are always a delicious treat.

Crust

> 1 cup Brown Rice Flour Mix (see p. 6)
> $\frac{1}{4}$ cup granulated sugar
> 1 teaspoon xanthan gum
> 5 tablespoons cold unsalted butter

1. Preheat oven to 350°F. Position rack in center of oven. Spray bottom of 8-inch square baking pan with cooking spray and generously dust with rice flour.

2. Put flour, sugar, and xanthan gum in large bowl of electric mixer; mix to blend. Add butter and mix on low speed until crumbly. Press dough into bottom of baking pan.

3. Bake in center of oven for 15 minutes or until very light golden.

Lemon Filling

> 3 large eggs
> $\frac{3}{4}$ cup granulated sugar
> 2 tablespoons Brown Rice Flour Mix (see p. 6)
> $\frac{1}{2}$ teaspoon baking powder
> $\frac{1}{8}$ teaspoon salt
> $\frac{1}{3}$ cup fresh lemon juice
> 2 teaspoons lemon rind
> $\frac{1}{2}$ teaspoon pure lemon extract
> Confectioner's sugar

1. Beat eggs in large bowl of electric mixer at high speed until foamy. Add sugar, flour, baking powder, salt, lemon juice, lemon rind, and lemon extract. Beat until well blended. Pour onto partially baked crust.

2. Bake in center of oven for 20 minutes or until set. Cool on wire rack. Cut into 16 squares or triangles; remove from baking pan onto serving plate. Sift confectioner's sugar over tops. Serve at room temperature or slightly chilled.

KEY LIME SQUARES

Substitute ⅓ cup Nellie & Joe's Key West Lime Juice (or other brand of key lime juice if this is not available. Regular lime juice is not the same) for lemon juice, and 2 teaspoons lime rind for lemon rind. Use lime extract, if available, instead of lemon extract.

Store any leftover lemon squares in a tightly sealed container in refrigerator. Do not freeze. Best when eaten within 4 days of baking.

ICE CREAM SANDWICHES

*Makes approximately
12 filled sandwiches*

Summer is the perfect season for ice cream sandwiches. But you have to admit, they are hard to find gluten-free. Now you can indulge in this old-fashioned favorite once again. They are easy to make and delicious. The cookie is full of rich chocolate flavor, with none of the chemical taste or preservatives of the store-bought variety. You get to choose the ice cream filling, so let your imagination soar with all the possibilities—mint choco-late chip, coffee, strawberry, toffee crunch, checkerboard of vanilla and chocolate. Cant wait? You won't miss those stale old ice cream sandwiches from the corner store ever again. Get baking!

*Unbaked dough can
be kept in refrigerator
for up to 3 days or
frozen for up to 2
months. To freeze,
wrap plastic-wrapped
log of dough in foil.*

$^3\!/_4$ cup unsalted butter

1 cup granulated sugar

1 large egg

1 teaspoon pure vanilla extract

1$^1\!/_2$ cups Brown Rice Flour Mix (see p. 6)

$^1\!/_2$ cup sweet rice flour

$^1\!/_2$ cup baking cocoa

1 teaspoon xanthan gum

1 teaspoon baking powder

1 teaspoon baking soda

$^1\!/_4$ teaspoon salt

Filling

Your favorite ice cream

1. Preheat oven to 350°F. Position rack in center of oven. Lightly grease cookie sheet with cooking spray.

2. Beat butter and sugar at medium speed in large bowl of electric mixer until well blended. Add egg and vanilla and beat well.

2. Add flours, baking cocoa, xanthan gum, baking powder, baking soda, and salt and mix until a soft dough is formed.

3. To shape into a square (for traditionally shaped ice cream sand-wiches), drop dough in a mound on large sheet of plastic wrap. Fold the plastic over the dough and shape into a long rectangle 6 inches long, 2 $^1\!/_2$ inches wide, and 2 $^1\!/_2$ inches high, using plastic to flatten ends. Try to smooth dough with your fingers. Refrigerate until well chilled.

4. Using a thin, sharp knife, slice chilled dough into $\frac{1}{4}$-inch-thick squares (2$\frac{1}{2}$ x 2$\frac{1}{2}$ inches) and place 1 inch apart on cookie sheet. Bake in center of oven for 11–12 minutes or until cooked through. (Cook 1–2 minutes extra for a crisper cookie.) Cool slightly on cookie sheet and transfer to wire rack to cool completely.

5. Cut ice cream into squares 1 to 1$\frac{1}{2}$ inches thick. Place each ice cream square on a cookie and cover each with another cookie. Wrap each sandwich in plastic wrap and store in airtight container in freezer. Cookies and ice cream can also be kept separately and assembled just before serving.

For round ice cream sandwiches: Mound dough on plastic wrap, fold the plastic over the dough, and shape it into a round log 3 inches in diameter and 6 inches long.

The edges of each ice cream sandwich can be dipped into tiny chocolate morsels, M&Ms, or other crushed candies for an extra added treat!

Store cookies in airtight container. After 3 days, store in refrigerator. Can be kept in refrigerator for 2 weeks or frozen for up to 1 month.

APPLE CRISP

Serves 6

If you find yourself yearning to use those apples you picked last weekend, consider making this delicious apple crisp. It is easy to prepare and keeps well in the refrigerator. I like to serve it warm for dessert with ice cream or frozen yogurt, but I also look forward to eating the leftovers cold for breakfast. I use a combination of apples, usually Granny Smith and Golden Delicious. But you can use any combination of cooking apples.

    1 cup Brown Rice Flour Mix (see p. 6)
    ¾ cup granulated sugar
    1¼ teaspoons baking powder
    1 teaspoon cinnamon
    ½ teaspoon xanthan gum
    ½ teaspoon salt
    1 large egg
    6 cups thinly sliced peeled apples
    ⅓ cup butter, melted

Store any leftovers tightly covered in refrigerator. Can be rewarmed in microwave.

1. Preheat oven to 350°. Position rack in center of oven. Lightly grease 9-inch round cake pan with cooking spray.

2. Combine flour, sugar, baking powder, cinnamon, xanthan gum, and salt in small bowl. Add egg and stir to mix well (mixture will be crumbly).

3. Place apples in cake pan and sprinkle top with flour mixture. Drizzle with melted butter.

4. Place cake pan in center of oven and bake about 40 minutes or until apples are tender and topping is a golden color. Serve warm.

PEAR CRISP

Substitute 6 cups thickly sliced peeled pears for apples.

SUMMER FRUIT CRISP
(PEACHES, APRICOTS, PLUMS, CHERRIES, OR BERRIES)

Serves 6

This is one of those desserts you can pull together in minutes, but it tastes like you spent hours. Try it when you have fresh ripe fruit from summer farm stands. In the winter you can use the new flash-frozen fruits available in grocery stores. Take note: Defrost frozen fruit in a colander so any liquid drains away before putting it in the pan.

5 heaping cups thinly sliced peeled fresh peaches (or other fruit)

⅓–½ cup granulated sugar

2 tablespoons Brown Rice Flour Mix (see p. 6)

½ teaspoon cinnamon

¼ teaspoon nutmeg

3 tablespoons lemon juice

Topping Mixture

1 cup Brown Rice Flour Mix (see p. 6)

½ cup brown sugar

½ teaspoon cinnamon

½ teaspoon xanthan gum

¼ teaspoon salt

⅓ cup unsalted butter, melted

Store any leftovers tightly covered in refrigerator for up to 3 days. Can be rewarmed in microwave.

1. Preheat oven to 375? F. Position rack in center of oven. Spray 9-inch deep-dish pie plate with cooking spray.

2. In large mixing bowl, toss peaches with sugar, flour, and spices until evenly coated. Stir in lemon juice. Pour peach mixture into prepared pie plate. Set aside.

3. Prepare topping mixture by combining flour, brown sugar, cinnamon, xanthan gum, and salt in a small bowl; stir to blend. Pour in butter, and stir until all dry ingredients are moistened. Break into small pieces with spoon. Apply topping mixture evenly over peaches and pat it firmly into place.

4. Bake in center of oven for about 40 minutes or until bubbly and brown. Serve warm with vanilla ice cream or yogurt.

PUMPKIN BREAD PUDDING WITH CARAMEL SAUCE

Serves 10

This bread pudding is delicious comfort food with a twist. The aroma of pumpkin and spices will fill your home and keep everyone glued to the table, ready for dessert. Needless to say, the leftovers are also good for breakfast. The trick for making a good gluten-free bread pudding is to use *good bread* and to toast it slightly in the oven. Don't waste good ingredients trying to make the best of those dense, hard, flavorless loaves of bread available in the freezer sections of food stores.

8 cups of gluten-free "plain white" bread cubes,* (about 1 lb.)

2 cups half-and-half

1 15-oz. can pumpkin puree

1 cup dark brown sugar

4 large eggs

1$\frac{1}{2}$ teaspoons cinnamon

$\frac{1}{2}$ teaspoon nutmeg

$\frac{1}{2}$ teaspoon ginger

$\frac{1}{2}$ teaspoon allspice

2 teaspoons pure vanilla extract

$\frac{1}{2}$ cup golden raisins

Confectioner's sugar

Caramel Sauce

$\frac{2}{3}$ cup dark brown sugar

$\frac{1}{4}$ cup unsalted butter

$\frac{1}{3}$ cup heavy cream

* You can make your own bread (see p. 129), using Bread Flour Mix A or Bread Flour Mix B, or you can use a fresh, top-quality rice bread that is not purchased frozen (such as Whole Foods' own Sandwich Bread). The small, hard-frozen rice breads will not make a good bread pudding.

1. Preheat oven to 325° F. Position rack in center of oven. Remove crusts from bread and cut into $\frac{1}{2}$-inch squares. Spread bread cubes on a large baking sheet and bake until cubes are dried out and light golden. Allow to cool thoroughly.

2. Preheat oven to 350°F. Lightly spray a glass or ceramic 11 x 7 x 2-inch baking dish with cooking spray.

3. Whisk half-and-half, pumpkin, brown sugar, eggs, spices, and vanilla extract in large bowl until smooth. Fold in bread cubes and raisins. Let sit for 30 minutes.

4. Pour mixture into prepared baking dish and place in center of oven. Bake about 40 minutes or until tester inserted into center of bread pudding comes out clean.

5. Prepare Caramel Sauce while bread pudding bakes. Whisk brown sugar and butter in heavy saucepan over medium-high heat until butter melts. Whisk in cream and stir until sugar dissolves and sauce is smooth, about 3 minutes. Keep warm.

6. Sift confectioner's sugar over finished bread pudding. Serve warm with Caramel Sauce.

Store any leftovers tightly covered in refrigerator. Can be rewarmed in microwave.

COCONUT BREAD PUDDING

Serves 10

Sweet coconut and crunchy pecans blend with a bit of pineapple to make this dessert something special. If you like coconut, this is one of those recipes you will make again and again. Serve it after spicy jambalayas and gumbos or tangy barbecues. Be sure to use a good quality gluten-free bread, and toast it slightly as instructed in the directions for the best results.

1 pound gluten-free "plain white" bread*

$\frac{1}{2}$ cup sweetened shredded coconut

1 cup pecans, chopped and lightly toasted**

1 cup crushed (canned) pineapple, drained

1 15-oz. can cream of coconut (Coco Lopez® or Goya®)

$2\frac{1}{2}$ cups whole milk

$\frac{1}{2}$ cup granulated sugar

6 large eggs

1 tablespoon pure vanilla extract

Confectioner's sugar

Store any leftovers tightly covered in refrigerator. Can be rewarmed in microwave.

* You can make your own bread, using Bread Flour Mix A or Bread Flour Mix B (see p. 129), or you can use a fresh, top-quality rice bread that is not purchased frozen (such as Whole Foods' own Sandwich Bread). The small, hard-frozen rice breads will not make a good bread pudding.

** Bake pecans about 5 minutes in preheated 350°F oven.

1. Preheat oven to 325° F. Position rack in center of oven. Remove crusts from bread and cut into 1-inch squares. Spread bread cubes on a large baking sheet, and bake until cubes are dried out and light golden. Allow to cool thoroughly.

2. Preheat oven to 350°F. Lightly spray glass or ceramic 13 x 9 x 2-inch baking dish with cooking spray.

3. Mix bread, sweetened shredded coconut, toasted pecans, and crushed pineapple together in a large bowl and set aside.

4. Combine cream of coconut, whole milk, and sugar in heavy medium-size saucepan. Stir over medium heat until sugar dissolves and mixture is warm. Remove from heat.

5. Whisk eggs in large bowl to blend. Whisk in warm milk mixture and vanilla. Pour mixture over breadcrumbs and mix in VERY gently. Let sit for 30 minutes.

6. Pour mixture into prepared baking dish. Gently push bread mixture into milk mixture. Bake in center of oven until pudding is set and golden brown, about 45 minutes. Cool slightly.

7. Sift confectioner's sugar over pudding. Serve warm.

CREAM PUFFS

Cream Puffs are an old-fashioned treat. You can fill them with sweetened whipped cream or creamy puddings such as Vanilla Filling (see p. 123), or you can make Profiteroles by filling them with a scoop of ice cream and resting them in a pool of chocolate sauce (recipes follow). Cream Puffs really aren't hard to make; just follow the detailed instructions below and in no time you will have a plate full of luscious cream puffs to share with family and friends. Take note: The baked puff paste dough freezes well, so double the recipe and make extra for the freezer. You'll have cream puff shells available to fill for fabulous last-minute desserts.

Make 8 puffs, 2 ½ to 3 inches diameter. Recipe can be doubled

$\frac{1}{2}$ cup Brown Rice Flour Mix (see p. 6)

1 teaspoon granulated sugar

$\frac{1}{8}$ teaspoon xanthan gum

$\frac{1}{8}$ teaspoon salt

$\frac{1}{4}$ cup unsalted butter, cut into 4 pieces

$\frac{1}{2}$ cup fat-free milk

$\frac{1}{2}$ teaspoon pure vanilla extract

2 large eggs

Vanilla Filling (see p. 123)

1. Preheat oven to 400°F. Position rack in center of oven. Line a large, heavy baking sheet with parchment paper.

2. Combine flour, sugar, xanthan gum, and salt in small bowl and set aside.

3. Bring butter and milk to a boil in a 1-quart saucepan over medium heat. Try not to allow too much of the milk to evaporate. As soon as the milk mixture boils, remove saucepan from heat and add flour mixture all at once. Use a soup spoon, and stir vigorously to combine. The dough should come together in a tight ball.

4. Return saucepan to a medium heat and cook, stirring constantly, until dough has a smooth appearance and oil from the butter begins to glisten on the surface (about 1 minute). The bottom of the pan will be coated with a thin film of dough, and the temperature of the inside of the dough taken with an instant-read thermometer should be 140°–150°F. (Use a thermometer; don't guess until you've done it many times!)

5. Transfer the dough to the large bowl of an electric mixer. Begin to beat dough at medium speed and add the vanilla and then the eggs one at a time; allow the first egg to be fully absorbed and the dough

to become smooth and shiny before adding the second. After each addition, the dough will separate into slippery little lumps before coming back together. Beat until dough is very smooth in consistency and is a very pale yellow color, about 2–3 minutes.

6. Use a pastry bag with a ½-inch smooth, round opening at the tip. Fill the pastry bag with warm dough. Squeeze the dough onto the prepared baking sheet, making circular mounds 2 inches in diameter and 1 inch high at the highest point. Space the mounds 2 inches apart. Be sure to tap down any pointy dough tips that result from pulling away the pastry bag from each mound.

7. Put baking sheet on center rack in oven and bake about 25 minutes or *until dough rises and puffs are double or triple in size and dough turns golden brown.* Turn oven temperature down to 300°F but do not open door. Bake another 8–10 minutes or until puffs are firm and crusty to the touch. Remove baking sheet from oven; turn oven off.

8. Quickly and carefully slice each puff in half horizontally with a thin, pointy knife; leave one side connected, if desired. Put the puffs back on the baking sheet with the two halves open. Put baking sheet back in oven with door ajar for about 10 minutes or until the interiors have dried out. Take note: If the puffs are moist inside, they will shrink. Cool completely on a rack before filling and serving.

Store in refrigerator until ready to serve. Best when eaten within 3 days of baking.

To use immediately:
Spoon desired filling into bottom half of puff and cover with top half. Sift confectioner's sugar over top if desired.

To use within 24 hours:
Store in an airtight container at room temperature. Recrisp in preheated 350°F oven. Allow to cool completely on a rack and fill as above.

To freeze for use within 2 weeks:
Store in an airtight container and freeze for up 2 weeks. Defrost, recrisp, cool, and fill as above.

PROFITEROLES

Fill cooled puffs with a scoop of vanilla or chocolate ice cream. To serve, spread warm chocolate sauce (recipe follows) on dessert plate and place profiteroles on top of sauce.

Chocolate sauce can be stored tightly covered in refrigerator for up to 3 weeks. Rewarm on stove or in microwave.

Chocolate Sauce
Combine ½ cup heavy cream, 1 tablespoon unsalted butter, and 2 tablespoons light corn syrup in a small, heavy saucepan. Bring to a boil, whisking constantly. Remove from heat. Add 4 ounces chopped semisweet chocolate and whisk until smooth. Makes 1 cup.

VANILLA FILLING
FOR CREAM PUFFS AND ECLAIRS

Makes about 2 ½ cups

    4 large egg yolks
    ⅔ cup granulated sugar
    ¼ cup cornstarch
    ¼ teaspoon salt
    2 cups whole milk
    1 tablespoon unsalted butter
    1–2 tablespoons pure vanilla extract*

1. Beat egg yolks in large bowl of electric mixer at medium-high speed until foamy. Gradually add sugar a little at a time, and continue beating until the mixture is pale yellow and thick. Add the cornstarch and salt and beat until well blended.

2. Bring milk to a boil in a large, heavy saucepan over medium-high heat while you are beating the egg yolks.

3. With the mixer on low, gradually add hot milk to egg mixture in a thin stream. Quickly scrape sides and bottom of bowl and mix at medium speed until well blended.

4. Pour the custard mixture back into the saucepan and cook it over medium-high heat, stirring constantly with a wire whip, until it comes to a boil and thickens. Lower heat and cook for 1 minute more. Remove from heat and beat in butter and vanilla.

5. Put custard in medium bowl or plastic container to cool. Cover top with plastic wrap to prevent a skin from forming over the surface, and chill in refrigerator.

Can be stored in refrigerator for up to 5 days or in freezer for up to 1 month in a tightly sealed container. Keep plastic wrap on surface.

* Optional flavoring for Cream Puffs: 1 tablespoon pure vanilla extract and 1–2 tablespoons rum, cognac, orange liqueur, or coffee-flavored liqueur.

* Optional flavoring for Eclairs: 1 tablespoon pure vanilla extract and 1 teaspoon (or to taste) pure almond extract.

LIGHTER VANILLA CREAM FILLING FOR CREAM PUFFS

Make half of Vanilla Filling recipe above. Beat 1 cup heavy cream in large bowl of electric mixer until stiff peaks form. Fold into prepared Vanilla Filling above.

ECLAIRS

*Makes 8 eclairs,
5 inches long.
Recipe can be doubled*

Eclairs are a special pastry dessert that convert well to gluten-free. You can double the recipe and make extra for the freezer because the baked puff paste dough actually freezes well. You can also make the eclairs larger than the directions detail below, but you will have to bake them longer. Before you do this, though, I suggest you make the recipe a few times following the directions exactly to get a feel for what the eclair should look like before you lower the temperature.

If you miss eating Cannoli—those delicious crisp Italian pastries filled with a creamy ricotta mixture—this recipe might help you out a bit. Make the pastry below but fill it with your favorite Cannoli filling. It won't be exactly what you remember, but it will help soothe the craving.

> $\frac{1}{2}$ cup Brown Rice Flour Mix (see p. 6)
>
> 1 teaspoon granulated sugar
>
> $\frac{1}{8}$ teaspoon xanthan gum
>
> $\frac{1}{8}$ teaspoon salt
>
> $\frac{1}{4}$ cup unsalted butter, cut into 4 pieces
>
> $\frac{1}{2}$ cup fat-free milk
>
> $\frac{1}{2}$ teaspoon pure vanilla extract
>
> 2 large eggs
>
> Chocolate Glaze (recipe follows)
>
> Vanilla Filling (see p. 123)

1. Preheat oven to 400°F. Position rack in center of oven. Line a large, heavy baking sheet with parchment paper.

2. Combine flour, sugar, xanthan gum, and salt in small bowl and set aside.

3. Bring butter and milk to a boil in a 1-quart saucepan over medium heat. Try not to allow too much of the milk to evaporate. As soon as the milk mixture boils, remove pan from heat and add flour mixture all at once. Use a soup spoon, and stir vigorously to combine. The dough should come together in a tight ball.

4. Return the pan to medium heat and cook, stirring constantly, until dough has a smooth appearance and oil from the butter begins to glisten on the surface (about 1 minute). The bottom of the pan will be coated with a thin film of dough, and the temperature of the inside of the dough taken with an instant-read thermometer should be 140°–150°F. (Use a thermometer—don't guess until you've done the recipe many times.)

5. Transfer the dough to the large bowl of an electric mixer. Begin to mix dough at medium speed and add the vanilla and then the eggs one at a time; allow the first egg to be fully absorbed and the dough to become smooth and shiny before adding the second. After each addition, the dough will separate into slippery little lumps before coming back together. Beat until dough is very smooth in consistency and is a very pale color (2–3 minutes.)

6. Use a pastry bag with a $\frac{1}{2}$-inch smooth, round opening at the tip. Fill the pastry bag with warm dough. Squeeze the dough onto the prepared baking sheet, making strips 4 inches long by 1 inch wide. Space the strips 2 inches apart. Be sure to tap down any pointy dough tips that result from pulling away the pastry bag from each mound.

7. Put baking sheet on center rack in oven and bake about 25 minutes *or until dough rises and eclairs are double or triple in size and dough turns rich golden brown.* Turn oven temperature down to 300°F but do not open door. Bake another 8–10 minutes or until eclairs are firm and crusty to the touch. Remove baking sheet from oven; turn oven off.

8. Quickly and carefully slice each eclair in half horizontally with a thin, pointy knife; leave one side connected, if desired. Put the eclairs back on the baking sheet with the two halves open. Put baking sheet back in oven with door ajar for about 10 minutes or until interiors have dried out. Take note: If the eclairs are moist inside, they will shrink. Cool completely on a rack before filling and serving.

To use immediately:
Spoon filling onto bottom half of eclair and cover with top half.

To use within 24 hours:
Store in an airtight container at room temperature. Recrisp in preheated 350°F oven. Allow to cool completely on a rack and fill as above.

To freeze for use within 2 weeks:
Store in an airtight container and freeze for up to 2 weeks. Defrost, recrisp, cool, and fill as above.

9. Spread a thick strip of Chocolate Glaze (recipe follows) down length of each eclair. Refrigerate until ready to serve. Best when eaten within 3 days of baking.

Glaze can be made ahead and rewarmed in microwave. Store tightly covered in refrigerator for up to 3 weeks.

Chocolate Glaze

2 ozs. semisweet chocolate

1½ tablespoons unsalted butter

1. Melt semisweet chocolate and butter in a small, heavy saucepan over medium-low heat; stir constantly until smooth. Immediately remove from heat and cool slightly. Makes about ⅓ cup.

Breads, Bread Crumbs, Pizza, and More

YOU PROBABLY ALREADY realize that you can no longer take bread for granted. Good gluten-free sandwich bread is hard to find. And finding a great loaf of gluten-free Italian or French bread, well, it's a journey filled with heartbreak. But you may find solace here. Although the wheat breads we are familiar with are clearly the most difficult to reproduce gluten-free, you can still make delicious bread. The recipes in this chapter do not compromise on tenderness for sandwich breads or crusty crusts and chewy interiors for European-style breads. Follow the directions carefully, and you will be able to find a new favorite or two.

And now a word about pizza. Even though you may have thought of pizza as a fast food, it never really was. The pizza maker in a *good* pizza parlor had been hard at work making the dough, cooking the sauce, and grating the cheese long before you got there. In fact, it would be safe to say that it took him longer to make that crust than it took you to drive over and pick up your pizza (or for them to deliver it to you). Good gluten-free pizza is definitely not fast food; it will take some thought and some prep time. But the pizza recipe in this book makes a fabulous pizza, and you will be happy when you eat it.

In spite of my warning, it really doesn't take long to make. Even better, you can prebake the crust; then when you are ready to eat, simply put on the sauce and cheese and finish baking the pizza in the oven.

There are several other tempting nontraditional bread recipes in this book for you to try, including a few special favorites from my house: Cheese Puffs and Walnut Bread.

This chapter uses the following pans:

• 8 ½ x 4 ½-inch loaf pan **(not non-stick!)**

• 9 x 5-inch loaf pan

• French bread pan, 4 inches wide, for Submarine Sandwich Bread

• French bread pan, 2 ½ inches wide, for French-Italian Bread

• 9-inch round cake pan

• 12-inch round pizza pan (with ridged bottom, not smooth) *or* 12-inch bottom of springform pan (with ridged bottom, not smooth)

• 9-inch round pizza pan (with ridged bottom, not smooth) *or* 9-inch bottom of springform pan (with ridged bottom, not smooth)

• Large, heavy baking sheets

THE LAST WORD ON BREADS

• Set-up before starting the recipe: assemble all ingredients

• Measure carefully (see Chapter 3)

• **Check the date on your yeast to make sure it is fresh.** The recipes in this book use dependable ¼ ounce packets of active dry yeast granules readily available in grocery stores

• When making bread, heat water to 110°F; lower temperatures will inhibit the rise and higher temperatures could kill the yeast. Be sure to mix the yeast in with the dry ingredients before adding the warm water (except in the bread crumb recipe)

• To create a warm place for your breads and pizza to rise, you can preheat your oven to 80°F, turn the oven off, put the bread or pizza dough inside, and then close the oven door. **If the oven is too warm, your bread will not rise correctly when you bake it!**

• Preheat the oven to the proper temperature (make sure the oven is calibrated correctly)

• Do not open the oven door more than necessary

• Use an instant read thermometer to check temperatures of liquids for breads, interiors of finished baked breads, and dough for Cheese Puffs

• Use a timer because you can get distracted

BASIC SANDWICH BREAD

Looking for a delicious sandwich bread? This loaf has the consistency of homemade white bread: It's not squishy like mass-produced bread, and it won't harden like a rock or become crumbly. You can make kid-friendly peanut butter and jelly sandwiches for a school lunch or scrumptious grilled cheese and Philly cheese steak sandwiches when you're near a stove. You can also make a yummy piece of buttered toast.

Take note: Allow the bread to rise slowly. Don't put it in a place that is too warm—the ideal temperature is about 80°F. A fast rise will contribute to an unstable bread that is likely to fall. The xanthan gum needs time to set in gluten-free breads. Also, try not to let the bread rise above the pan before you bake it because this will also contribute to instability.

> 2 large eggs (room temperature is best)
> 3 tablespoons canola oil
> 2 cups Bread Flour Mix A, B, or C (see p. 8)
> 1½ teaspoons xanthan gum
> ½ teaspoon salt
> 1 teaspoon unflavored gelatin
> 2 tablespoons sugar
> 1 packet (¼ oz.) of active dry yeast granules (not quick rise)
> ¾ cup plus 2 tablespoons fat-free milk, heated to 110°F

1. Lightly grease and flour an 8½ x 4½-inch loaf pan — not non-stick (use approximately ½ teaspoon plain rice flour).

2. Mix eggs and canola oil together in a small bowl and set aside.

3. Mix all dry ingredients in large bowl of electric mixer. Quickly add warm milk and egg and oil mixture to the bowl; mix until just blended. Scrape bowl and beaters, and then beat at high speed for 3 minutes. Spoon dough into prepared pan; cover and let rise in a warm place for 30–40 minutes or until dough just reaches ½ inch below top of pan. If you use a warm 80°F oven to help the bread rise, and you have only one oven, you will have to pull the bread out before it is finished rising in order to preheat the oven to bake it.

4. Place rack in center of oven. Preheat oven to 400°F while bread is rising (do not use a convection oven; bread will brown too quickly).

5. Bake bread in center of preheated oven for 10 minutes; cover with aluminum foil and bake another 40–45 minutes. Bread should have a hollow sound when tapped on the sides and bottom. Instant read thermometer should register about 195°F–200°F. Remove bread from oven and turn onto a rack to cool.

Makes one 1-lb. loaf

Wrap bread well in plastic wrap and then foil. Store in refrigerator for up to 1 week or freezer for up to 3 weeks.

Cook's Notes: Dry ingredients can be mixed ahead and stored in plastic containers for future use. But do not add yeast until just ready to bake bread.

For sandwiches kids will like, use ¼ cup sweet rice flour and 1¾ cups Bread Flour Mix to get a "softer" bread.

BREAD CRUMBS

Makes about 8 cups

Bread crumbs are an important part of many dishes, and you probably won't want to be without them in your pantry. My simple recipe uses potato starch and cornstarch to make an inexpensive, bland bread that is ground into almost 8 cups of bread crumbs. (You do the math! Compare this to the price of gluten-free bread crumbs in the store.) Yeast flavors the bread, but baking powder is used for a quick rise. The loaf isn't really delicious to eat as bread, but it makes a fabulous bread crumb that you will love to cook with. You can also toast the crumbs in the oven (see Cook's Note in margin) or toss them with herbs and spices to make flavored bread crumbs of your choosing.

Cook's Note: For toasted bread crumbs: Preheat oven to 325°F. Spread bread crumbs out on shallow baking pan and place in center of oven. Stir every few minutes until desired color is reached.

- 1 cup milk, heated to 105°F
- 1 packet (¼ oz.) of dry quick-rise yeast granules
- 1¼ cups potato starch
- 1¼ cups cornstarch
- 1 teaspoon xanthan gum
- 1 tablespoon baking powder
- ½ teaspoon salt
- 2 tablespoons sugar
- 1 large egg
- ¼ cup canola oil

1. Arrange rack in center of oven and preheat to 350°F. Lightly grease a 9 x 4-inch loaf pan.

2. Stir yeast into warmed milk (105°F) and set aside.

3. Mix all dry ingredients together in bowl of electric mixer. Add egg, canola oil, and milk/yeast mixture to dry ingredients; mix until just blended. Scrape bowl and beaters and beat on medium speed for 1 minute. Dough will be thick.

4. Spoon dough into prepared pan and place on rack in center of oven. Bake 30–35 minutes or until toothpick inserted into center of loaf comes out dry. Instant read thermometer should register 195°F. Loaf will be a very light brown.

5. Remove bread from oven and turn onto a rack to cool completely. Cut into thin slices and grind in an electric blender or food processor until fine crumbs appear. Store in a tightly sealed container in freezer.

FRENCH-ITALIAN BREAD

I never thought I would be able to eat a piece of French or Italian bread again. But I was hungry for the fragrant loaves I had to leave behind. Although this one is missing the flavor of wheat, it has a great crunchy crust and a chewy interior that comes closer than any store-bought gluten-free loaf or recipe I've tried. If you want to darken the crust color, spray the loaf with a *light mist* of canola oil (or canola baking spray) before you put it in the oven. You can sprinkle it with sesame seeds to add a little extra flavor, or you can come to depend on the delicious nuttiness of the millet flour to stand in for the lack of wheat. Not a bad option either way. Grab a hunk of fabulous cheese and a bottle of wine and make a loaf today.

Makes one 14 x 3-inch loaf or two 7 x 3-inch loaves. Recipe can be doubled

2 cups Bread Flour Mix A* (see p. 8)

1¼ teaspoons xanthan gum

¾–1 teaspoon salt (to taste)

4 teaspoons sugar

1 packet (¼ oz.) of active dry yeast granules (not quick rise)

2 teaspoons olive oil

1 cup water, heated to 110°F

1. Lightly spray a 2½-inch-wide French bread loaf pan with baking spray and dust lightly with white rice flour (spray and dust it over a paper towel if the pan has little holes in it).

2. Mix all dry ingredients in large bowl of electric mixer. Quickly add olive oil and warm water (110°F) to the bowl; mix until just blended. Scrape bowl and beaters, and then beat at high speed for 3 minutes. Spoon dough into prepared pan; cover with a light cloth and let rise in a warm place (80°F is ideal) for 40–50 minutes or until dough has slightly more than doubled in size.

3. Place rack in center of oven. Preheat oven to 400°F while bread is rising (do not use a convection oven because it will brown the bread too quickly).

4. Bake bread in center of preheated oven for 40–50 minutes (35–45 minutes for two smaller loaves). When done, bread should have a hollow sound when tapped on the sides. Instant read thermometer should register 205–215°F. You can bake it longer to make a thicker crust; the color will deepen and the internal temperature will continue to rise. Remove bread from pan and cool on a rack at least 15 minutes before slicing. The crust will soften a bit after the bread cools, but you can easily recrisp it in the oven.

Loaves can be stored in refrigerator for up to 3 days or freezer for up to 3 weeks; wrap well in plastic wrap and then foil. Rewarm in 350°F preheated oven; wrap in foil if you do not want a crisp crust (but open the foil for the last 5 minutes).

Cook's Note: Dry ingredients can be mixed ahead and stored in plastic containers for future use. But do not add yeast until just ready to bake bread.

* The recipe specifies Bread Flour Mix A, but you can also use Bread Flour Mix B, in which case the bread will be blander in flavor and lighter in color.

SUBMARINE SANDWICH BREAD

Perhaps you've been craving the sort of chewy, crusty sandwich bread used to make a meatball hero, roast beef sub, or muffuletta. Hero, wedge, sub, hoagie, grinder—you name it and you can make it with this bread. Shape the dough into a loaf big enough for two to share or into several smaller, individual sandwich rolls (perfect for small-kid lunches). It is simple to make: Just mix the ingredients in an electric mixer, put the dough in a French bread pan, and let it rise. It bakes up to a nice light golden brown, and you can use it to make any sandwich you're hungry for. If you want to darken the crust color, spray the loaf with a *light mist* of canola oil (or canola baking spray) before you put it in the oven.

Makes two 8 x 3-inch loaves, three 5 $\frac{1}{2}$ x 2 $\frac{1}{2}$-inch loaves, or one 12 x 3-inch loaf. Recipe can be doubled

The recipe specifies Bread Flour Mix A, but you can also use Bread Flour Mix B, in which case the bread will be blander in flavor and lighter in color.

1 $\frac{1}{2}$ cups Bread Flour Mix A* (see p. 8)
1 teaspoon xanthan gum
$\frac{3}{4}$ teaspoon salt
2 tablespoons sugar
1 packet ($\frac{1}{4}$ oz.) of active dry yeast granules (not quick rise)
1 teaspoon olive oil
$\frac{3}{4}$ cup plus 1 tablespoon water, heated to 110°F

1. Lightly spray a 4-inch-wide French bread loaf pan(s) with baking spray and dust lightly with white rice flour or sprinkle with corn-meal (spray and dust it over a paper towel if the pan has little holes in it).

2. Mix all dry ingredients in large bowl of electric mixer. Pour warm water (110°F) and olive oil into mixing bowl; mix until just blended. Scrape bowl and beaters and then beat at high speed for 2 minutes.

3. Spoon dough into prepared pan(s) and spread it out. Cover with a light cloth and let rise in a warm place (about 80°F) for 40–50 minutes or until dough has slightly more than doubled in size.

4. Place rack in lower third of oven. Preheat oven to 400°F while bread is rising (do not use a convection oven because it will brown the bread too quickly).

5. Bake bread in center of preheated oven for 35–45 minutes. Bread should have a hollow sound when tapped on the sides. Instant read thermometer should register 205–215°F. Bread should be light golden

in color. You can bake it longer to make a thicker crust; the color will deepen and the internal temperature will continue to rise. Remove bread from pan and cool on a rack at least 15 minutes before slicing. The crust will soften a bit after the bread cools, but you can easily recrisp it in the oven.

Loaves can be stored in refrigerator for up to 2 days or freezer for up to 3 weeks; wrap well in plastic wrap and then foil. Rewarm in 350°F preheated oven; wrap in foil if you do not want a crisp crust (but open the foil for the last 5 minutes).

Cook's Notes: Dry ingredients can be mixed ahead and stored in plastic containers for future use. But do not add yeast until just ready to bake bread.

RUSTIC FLAT BREAD
(FOCACCIA)

*Makes one 8- or 9-inch
round bread.
Recipe can be doubled*

Rustic flat breads can be found in cultures and cuisines around the globe. This one is more European in style, like the focaccia you find in Italian restaurants, specialty shops, and even grocery stores. I top mine in the classic way with olive oil, fresh rosemary, and sea salt. But let your imagination go: sweet sautéed onion and peppers, fresh tomatoes, olives, a little cheese. Try your old favorites or create new ones. This very-easy-to-make bread will become a favorite.

*Bread can be prepared
in advance: bake
according to directions.
Remove from oven
and allow to cool on
a rack. Wrap well in
plastic wrap and
then foil. Store in
refrigerator for up to
2 days or freezer for up
to 3 weeks. Rewarm in
350°F preheated oven;
wrap in foil if you do
not want a crisp crust
(but open the foil for
the last 5 minutes).*

*Cook's Note: Dry
ingredients can be
mixed ahead and
stored in plastic
containers for future
use. But do not add
yeast until just ready
to bake bread.*

** The recipe specifies
Bread Flour Mix A, but
you can also use Bread
Flour Mix B, in which
case the bread will be
blander in flavor and
lighter in color.*

$1\frac{1}{2}$ cups Bread Flour Mix A* (see p. 8)

1 teaspoon xanthan gum

$\frac{1}{2}$ teaspoon salt

1 tablespoon sugar

1 packet ($\frac{1}{4}$ oz.) of dry quick-rise yeast granules

1 teaspoon olive oil

$\frac{3}{4}$ cup plus 1 tablespoon water, heated to 110°F

Olive oil

Fresh rosemary

Sea salt

1. Spray an 8- or 9-inch round cake pan with baking spray and lightly dust with white rice flour or sprinkle with cornmeal.

2. Mix all dry ingredients in large bowl of electric mixer. Pour warm water (110°F) and olive oil into mixing bowl; mix until just blended. Scrape bowl and beaters, and then beat at high speed for 2 minutes.

3. Spoon dough into prepared pan and spread it out to the sides with a spatula. Cover with a light cloth and let rise in a warm place (about 80°F) for about 40 minutes. Bread should be approximately double in height.

4. Place rack in lower third of oven. Preheat oven to 400°F while bread is rising.

5. Sprinkle olive oil over top and carefully spread it into a *thin* film over the entire surface of the bread (use your fingers to do this for best results). Sprinkle with rosemary and sea salt (or other toppings of your choice).

6. Bake bread for about 20 minutes, about 15 minutes for 9-inch bread. Bread should be light golden in color and cooked through. Remove bread from pan and cool on a rack for 15 minutes; slice and serve.

PIZZA CRUST

This is the crust you have been waiting for. You won't even miss the wheat, and it's so good you will be able to serve it to anyone. It is a classic New York-style thin crust, but you could make it thicker by baking it in a smaller pan (be sure to adjust the baking time). Ideally, try to make the crust several hours or the day before you plan to use it. This gives the xantham gum time to set, and the crust will be crisp and chewy like one made with wheat. If you make the crust just before you use it, it will still be delicious and the texture will still be wonderful, but the crisp and chewy aspect won't be as pronounced. Prebaked crusts freeze well, so you can make several and store them in the freezer.

1 cup Brown Rice Flour Mix (see p. 6)

$\frac{1}{2}$ cup millet flour*

1 teaspoon xanthan gum

$\frac{1}{2}$ teaspoon salt

2 teaspoons sugar

1 packet ($\frac{1}{4}$ oz.) of dry quick-rise yeast granules

1 teaspoon olive oil

$\frac{3}{4}$ cup plus 1 tablespoon water, heated to 110°F

Cornmeal (optional)

1. Generously spray pizza pan(s) (with ridged bottom, not smooth) or bottom of springform pan(s) (with ridged bottoms, not smooth) with baking spray and lightly sprinkle cornmeal over entire pan (cornmeal is optional).

2. Mix all dry ingredients in large bowl of electric mixer. Pour olive oil and warm water (110°F) into mixing bowl; mix until just blended. Scrape bowl and beaters, and then beat at high speed for 2 minutes.

3. Spoon dough into center of prepared pan(s). Use a cake spatula to move dough from center to outer rim of pan using individual strokes; lightly dampen spatula with warm water as necessary. Try to arrange dough so that it covers entire pan in an even, thin layer. Cover with a light cloth and let rise in a warm place for 30–40 minutes. Pizza crust should approximately double in height.

4. Place rack in lower third of oven. Preheat oven to 425°F while pizza is rising.

5. Bake pizza in pan on rack of preheated oven for 15–16 minutes (12–14 minutes for 9-inch pizza). Pizza should be light golden in

Makes one 12-inch round pizza or two very thin 9-inch round pizzas. Recipe can be doubled

Cook's Note: Dry ingredients can be mixed ahead and stored in plastic containers for future use. But do not add yeast until just ready to bake pizza.

color and cooked through. Remove from oven and cover with pizza topping of your choice (make sure topping is not too wet).

6. Leave pizza in pan and return to oven for an additional 10 minutes (8 minutes for 9-inch crust). Remove pizza from pan and place it directly on rack for 6 minutes (4 minutes for 9-inch crust) to finish baking. Remove from oven, let rest 3 minutes, slice, and serve.

✳ ALTERNATIVE CRUST WITHOUT MILLET FLOUR
(CRUST WILL SHRINK UP TO 2 INCHES)

$1\frac{1}{2}$ cups Brown Rice Flour Mix (see p. 6)
1 teaspoon xanthan gum
$\frac{1}{2}$ teaspoon salt
2 teaspoons sugar
1 packet ($\frac{1}{4}$ oz.) of dry quick-rise yeast granules
1 teaspoon olive oil
$\frac{3}{4}$ cup plus 1 tablespoon water, heated to 110°F
Cornmeal (optional)

1. Follow directions for Pizza Crust, p. 135.

For softer crust:
Put on pizza topping and return pan to rack in lower third of oven; bake 15–20 minutes or until topping is cooked.

For very crisp crust:
Put on pizza topping, remove pizza from pan, and place pizza directly on rack in lower third of oven; bake 8–10 minutes (5–8 minutes for 9-inch pies) until topping is cooked and bottom is crispy.

Pizza crust can be prepared in advance: Precook crust according to directions, but do not put on topping. Remove from oven and allow crust to cool on a rack. Wrap well in plastic wrap and then foil. Store in refrigerator for up to 2 days or freezer for up to 3 weeks. Defrost crust before topping with sauce and cheese.

WALNUT BREAD

This fragrant quick-bread will win you over. It is the perfect choice if you are looking for something special to serve with a salad or cheese course at dinner. It has an uncommon crunchy texture and warm, nutty flavor that's not too sweet. You can toast it right before you serve it or several hours before and then warm the pieces briefly in a microwave. Walnut Bread freezes well, so you can make it ahead of time and then pull pieces out of the freezer to toast when you need them. I leave it in chunks several inches wide, which I defrost and then slice; it stays a little fresher tasting when left in larger pieces.

> 2 cups Brown Rice Flour Mix (see p. 6)
> ⅓ cup granulated sugar
> 1 tablespoon baking powder
> 1 teaspoon baking soda
> ¾ teaspoon xanthan gum
> ½ teaspoon salt
> 1 cup milk less 1 tablespoon
> ⅓ cup canola oil less 1 tablespoon
> 1 large egg
> ½ teaspoon pure vanilla extract
> 2 cups shelled walnuts, toasted and coarsely chopped*

1. Preheat oven to 350°F. Position rack in center of oven. Lightly grease 9 x 5-inch loaf pan with cooking spray.

2. Combine flour, sugar, baking powder, baking soda, xanthan gum, and salt in a large mixing bowl.

3. Combine milk, oil, egg, and vanilla in a small bowl and whisk until well blended.

4. Add milk mixture to flour mixture all at once and mix just until moistened. Fold in toasted nuts. Spoon batter into prepared pan.

5. Bake 30–35 minutes or until a toothpick inserted in center comes out clean. Cool for 5 minutes in pan. Remove from pan and cool completely on a wire rack.

To make toasted Walnut Bread slices:
Place rack in lower third of oven and preheat to 375°F. Slice bread into ¾-inch slices. Arrange in a single layer on a baking sheet. Bake for 8–10 minutes or until browned. Turn slices over and bake another 8–10 minutes until other side is browned. Serve with salad or cheese course.

*Makes one
9 x 5-inch loaf*

Walnut Bread can be prepared in advance: Bake according to directions. Remove from oven and allow to cool on a rack. Wrap well in plastic wrap and then foil. Store in refrigerator for up to 2 days or freezer for up to 3 weeks. Defrost and then toast bread slices.

* Cook's Note: Toast nuts on a baking sheet in preheated 350°F oven for 4–6 minutes.

BUTTERMILK BISCUITS

Makes five 2 1/2-inch round biscuits. Recipe can be doubled

When you're hungry for hot, buttery biscuits, nothing else will do. These buttermilk biscuits are crisp on the outside and tender on the inside. They are light but bursting with buttery flavor. Serve them hot from the oven with jam for breakfast, or use them to top a pot pie or fruit cobbler (add an extra tablespoon of sugar for a sweeter dessert biscuit). They are so delicious you can even serve them plain alongside soups and stews. Be sure to use extra-finely ground brown rice flour and sweet rice flour or your biscuits will be crumbly and not rise well. The grind of the flour will make a noticeable difference.

Biscuits can be stored in refrigerator for up to 2 days in an airtight container. Rewarm in 350°F pre-heated oven. Do not use a microwave.

  ³⁄₄ cup Brown Rice Flour Mix (see p. 6)

  ¹⁄₄ cup sweet rice flour

  2 teaspoons sugar

  2 teaspoons baking powder

  ¹⁄₄ teaspoon baking soda

  ¹⁄₄ teaspoon xanthan gum

  1 tablespoon buttermilk powder

  ¹⁄₄ teaspoon salt

  5 tablespoons cold unsalted butter, cut into 5 slices

  1 large egg white

  3 tablespoons water

1. Preheat oven to 425°. Position rack in center of oven. Spray small baking sheet with cooking spray and set aside.

2. Mix brown rice flour mix, sweet rice flour, sugar, baking powder, baking soda, xanthan gum, buttermilk powder, and salt in large bowl of electric mixer. With mixer on low speed, cut butter into flour mixture until mixture is crumbly and resembles coarse meal. Put mixture into a small bowl and set aside.

3. Beat egg white in the same large bowl of electric mixer until *very foamy*. Add water and flour mixture all at once, and mix at medium-low speed for 1 minute. Use lightly floured hands to pat out dough into a large ³⁄₄-inch-thick round on lightly floured surface. Cut out biscuits with a 2 ¹⁄₂-inch round cookie cutter. Press dough scraps together and repeat.

4. Place baking sheet on center rack of oven and turn oven temperature down to 400°F. Bake 15–18 minutes or until medium golden brown. Serve immediately.

CHEESE PUFFS

Make a batch of these cheese puffs for your next gathering, and watch them disappear before you even set them down. Cheese Puffs smell so good when they're baking in the oven that your guests will be circling around your kitchen waiting for them to come out. Add your favorite cheese to this puff paste dough, pipe it onto a cookie sheet, and then into the oven it goes. You can make the puffs ahead of time and simply reheat them for more effortless entertaining; just follow the directions for reheating below.

Makes 24 cheese puffs, 1 $\frac{1}{2}$ inches diameter. Recipe can be doubled

$\frac{1}{2}$ cup Brown Rice Flour Mix (see p. 6)

$\frac{1}{4}$ teaspoon xanthan gum

$\frac{1}{8}$ teaspoon salt

Dash finely ground pepper

Pinch nutmeg (optional)

$\frac{1}{4}$ cup unsalted butter, cut into 4 pieces

$\frac{1}{2}$ cup fat-free milk

2 large eggs

$\frac{1}{2}$ cup packed, grated Swiss, Gruyère, Cheddar, and/or Parmesan cheese

1. Preheat oven to 400°F. Position rack in center of oven. Line a large, heavy baking sheet with parchment paper.

2. Combine flour, xanthan gum, salt, pepper, and nutmeg (if using) in small bowl and set aside.

3. Bring butter and milk to a boil in a 1-quart saucepan over medium heat. Try not to allow too much milk to evaporate. As soon as milk mixture boils, remove pan from heat and add flour mixture all at once. Use a soup spoon to stir vigorously to combine. The dough should come together in a tight ball.

4. Return the pan to medium heat and cook, stirring constantly, until dough has a smooth appearance and oil from the butter begins to glisten on the surface (about 1 minute). Bottom of pan will be coated with a thin film of dough, and temperature inside the dough (taken with an instant-read thermometer) should be 140°–150°F. (Use a thermometer—don't guess until you've done it many times!)

5. Transfer dough to large bowl of an electric mixer. Begin to beat dough at medium speed while adding eggs one at a time; allow first egg to be fully absorbed and the dough to become smooth and shiny before adding second. After each addition, dough will separate into

slippery little lumps before coming back together. Beat until dough is very smooth in consistency and a very pale yellow color, about 2–3 minutes. Beat cheese into the warm dough.

6. Use a pastry bag with a $\frac{1}{2}$-inch smooth, round opening at the tip. Fill pastry bag with warm dough. Squeeze dough onto prepared baking sheet, making circular mounds 1 inch in diameter and $\frac{1}{2}$ inch high at highest point. Space mounds 2 inches apart. Be sure to tap down any pointy dough tips that result from pulling away the pastry bag. Sprinkle each cheese puff with a pinch of additional cheese if desired.

7. Place baking sheet on center rack in oven and bake about 20 minutes or until dough rises and turns medium golden brown. Turn oven temperature down to 300°F but do not open door. Bake another 5–10 minutes. Puffs are done when they have doubled or tripled in size, are a rich golden brown, and are firm and crusty to the touch. Remove baking sheet from oven and pierce side of each puff with a sharp knife to allow steam to escape.

To use immediately:
Serve cheese puffs immediately or at room temperature.

To use within 24 hours:
Store in an airtight container at room temperature. Puffs will soften. Recrisp in preheated 350°F oven.

To freeze for use within 2 weeks:
Store in an airtight container and freeze for up 2 weeks. Puffs will soften. Defrost and recrisp in preheated 350°F oven.

MEASUREMENTS/EQUIVALENTS

APPROXIMATE MEASUREMENTS

1 lemon = 3 tablespoons juice

1 lemon = 1 teaspoon grated peel

1 orange = $\frac{1}{3}$ cup juice

1 orange = 2 teaspoons grated peel

1 pound unshelled walnuts = $1\frac{1}{2}$ to $1\frac{3}{4}$ cups shelled

1 pound unshelled almonds = $\frac{3}{4}$ to 1 cup shelled

8 to 10 egg whites = 1 cup

12 to 14 egg yolks = $1\frac{1}{2}$ cups

EQUIVALENTS

3 teaspoons = 1 tablespoon

2 tablespoons = $\frac{1}{8}$ cup

4 tablespoons = $\frac{1}{4}$ cup

8 tablespoons = $\frac{1}{2}$ cup

16 tablespoons = 1 cup

5 tablespoons + 1 teaspoon = $\frac{1}{3}$ cup

12 tablespoons = $\frac{3}{4}$ cup

4 ounces = $\frac{1}{2}$ cup

8 ounces = 1 cup

$\frac{5}{8}$ cup = $\frac{1}{2}$ cup + 2 tablespoons

$\frac{7}{8}$ cup = $\frac{3}{4}$ cup + 2 tablespoons

16 ounces = 1 pound

1 ounce = 2 tablespoons fat or liquid

2 cups = 1 pint

2 pints = 1 quart

1 quart = 4 cups

speck = less than $\frac{1}{8}$ teaspoon

INDEX